# Modern World Religions

# Hinduism

Lynne Gibson

Heinemann Educational Publishers
Halley Court, Jordan Hill, Oxford, OX2 8EJ
Part of Harcourt Limited

Heinemann is the registered trademark of Harcourt
Education Limited

First published in 2002

06 05 04
10 9 8 7 6 5 4 3

**British Library Cataloguing in Publication Data**
A catalogue record for this book is available from the
British Library

ISBN 0 435 33619 3

Picture research by Jennifer Johnson
Typeset by Artistix, Thame, Oxon
Illustrated by Andrew Skilleter
Printed and bound in Spain by Edelvives

**Acknowledgements**
The publishers would like to thank the following for
permission to use photographs:

Andes Press Agency/Carlos Reyes-Manzo, p. 40 (left);
The Art Archive/British Library, pp. 18 (left), 19; The Art
Archive/Marco Polo Gallery Paris/Dagli Orti, p. 15; The
Art Archive/Victoria and Albert Museum London, p. 16;
Bhaktivedanta Manor, p. 53; Bruce Coleman Collection/
Alain Compost, p. 29; Circa Photo Library, pp. 4, 5 (bottom),
6, 17, 40 (right); Circa Photo Library/William Holtby, pp.
23, 35; Circa Photo Library/Bipin J. Mistry, pp. 11, 25, 32;
Circa Photo Library/John Smith, pp. 22, 38; Hulton
Archive/Peter Ruhe, p. 55; Panos Pictures/James Bedding,
p. 57; Science Photo Library/Francis Leroy, Biocosmos,
p. 56; TRIP/Dinodia, p. 8; TRIP/F. Good, pp. 46, 47, 52;
TRIP/R. Graham, p. 3; TRIP/S. Harris, p. 58; TRIP/H. Luther,
pp. 39, 45; TRIP/H. Rogers, pp. 5 (top), 12, 14, 18 (right),
20 (both) 21 (bottom), 27, 28 (both), 29 (bottom), 30, 31,
34, 43.

The publishers have made every effort to contact
copyright holders. However, if any material has been
incorrectly acknowledged, the publishers would be
pleased to correct this at the earliest opportunity.

**Websites**
Links to appropriate websites are given throughout the
pack. Although these were up to date at the time of
writing, it is essential for teachers to preview these sites
before using them with pupils. This will ensure that the
web address (URL) is still accurate and the content is
suitable for your needs. We suggest that you bookmark
useful sites and consider enabling pupils to access them
through the school intranet. We are bringing this to your
attention as we are aware of legitimate sites being
appropriated illegally by people wanting to distribute
unsuitable and offensive material. We strongly advise
you to purchase suitable screening software so that
pupils are protected from unsuitable sites and their
material. If you do find that the links given no longer
work, or the content is unsuitable, please let us know.
Details of changes will be posted on our website.

Tel: 01865 888058  www.heinemann.co.uk

# Contents

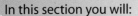

# *An introduction to Hinduism*

In this section you will:

● learn how Hinduism began and developed

● have the opportunity to reflect upon and explore some of the issues raised, such as why you think there are so many different religions in the world.

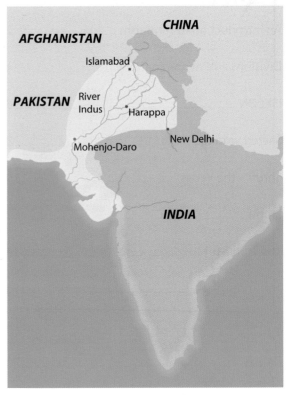

*A map of India showing the area where Hinduism began and developed*

## What is Hinduism?

**Hinduism** is the oldest major world religion. It is also the third largest religious tradition. About 900 million people are thought to be Hindus. Hinduism is the traditional religion of India, and Hindu communities can be found in many other countries. Most Hindus prefer to call their religion **Sanatan Dharma**, which means the 'eternal or imperishable religion'. They call their religion this because they believe that it is based on **divine**, or God-given, truths or laws that have always existed. Hindus say that Sanatan Dharma is not just a religion, it is a way of life for everyone, based on universal principles.

## How did Hinduism begin and develop?

No one knows exactly how and when Hinduism began. It has no single founder, which means that it is not based on the life or teachings of a particular person or group of people. Modern Hinduism is a collection of beliefs and practices that has developed over thousands of years. Hinduism has taken many of its ideas from the Vedic scriptures. The Vedic scriptures are a collection of Hindu **sacred** writings called the **Vedas**.

Traditionally, Hinduism has been very tolerant of other religions. Hindus have a saying, 'Ekam Sataha Vipraha Bahudha Vadanti', which can be translated as 'The truth is one, but different sages call it by different names.' They believe that many religions eventually lead to God even though the routes people take may be different.

Most people agree that Hinduism began in Northern India more than 5000 years ago. Some say it came into being when two ancient civilizations combined some of their religious beliefs and practices. These were the Dravidians, who lived in the Indus Valley in northern India, and the Aryans, who invaded India from the areas now known as central Asia and southern Russia. Some modern scholars are now questioning this theory, because traditional accounts of history can vary.

*Excavations showing the great bath at Mohenjo-Daro, an ancient settlement in the Indus Valley, northern India*

There are a number of different theories about where the terms 'Hinduism' and 'Hindu' come from. One idea is that they come from a Persian word 'Sindhu'. The country we now call Iran was once called Persia. In the Middle Ages, invaders from this country used the term 'Sindhu' to describe non-Muslims living around the River Indus in northern India. Over time, 'Sindhu' changed to 'Hindu' and was used to describe a family of religious and cultural traditions.

## Learning about religion

❶ Prepare a presentation to give to your class on the origins of Hinduism.

❷ Research how other religions began and developed, and find out how many followers they have. Compare and contrast your findings with Hinduism. Use the Internet to help you with your research.

❸ Describe the Hindu attitude towards other religions and explain why you think Hindus hold this view.

## Learning from religion

❶ Discuss in groups why you think there are so many different religions in the world.

❷ Make a list of things you believe to always be true no matter what the circumstances. Compare your ideas with the views of others in your class.

❸ Draw a flow chart or diagram showing some of the different routes people might take to find out about God.

# *Divisions and denominations*

In this section you will:

● learn how Hinduism is divided into different groups and look at the main Hindu denominations

● have the opportunity to reflect upon and write about some of the issues raised, such as the different characteristics, features and functions people might associate with God.

## Who is a Hindu?

**Hinduism** is a very diverse religion. All Hindus share some common beliefs but there is also a wide range of different practices within the religion covering every aspect of a Hindu's life. This is because Hinduism is more demanding about practice than theory. According to the Indian Supreme Court in 1995, a Hindu is someone who:

● accepts that the **Vedas**, **sacred** Hindu scriptures, contain the words of God

● recognizes that there are many different ways to know God

● realizes that there are a number of different **deities** that can be worshipped.

## What are the main divisions and denominations within Hinduism?

Hinduism is a **monotheistic** religion. Hindus believe in one God, an underlying spirit, which they call Brahman. Many Hindus believe that the different characteristics, features and functions of Brahman can be represented by the various deities whom they worship.

Hinduism is also a **henotheistic** religion. This means that some followers believe that one deity represents the Supreme God and that the other deities are secondary.

There are many different groups, or **denominations**, within Hinduism. Most Hindus belong to one of three main denominations. The denomination they belong to depends upon which deity they have chosen to worship. Smaller groups then usually follow the teachings of a particular holy man, also known as a **guru** or **swami**.

### Vaishnavism

Hindus who belong to this denomination have chosen to worship Vishnu and his **avatars**, or incarnations, the most popular of which is Krishna. This is the largest group within Hinduism and about 80 per cent of Hindus are **Vaishnavas**.

*Krishna, an avatar of Vishnu, the most popular Hindu deity*

## Shaivism

Hindus who belong to this denomination have mainly chosen to worship the deity Shiva. People who worship Shiva are called **Shaivas**.

## Shaktas

The **Shaktas** worship Shakta, the wife of Shiva. Shakta has many different forms, such as Devi, Mataji, Parvati, Durga, Kali and Amba. Shaktism may also include the worship of other female deities, most specifically Lakshmi and Saraswati.

Generally, especially in India, most Hindus who live in towns are either Vaishnavas or Shaivas. Hindus who live in rural areas tend to worship a female deity.

*Shiva, a member of the **Trimurti**: the deity of destruction and a reproductive power*

*Kali, a form of Shakti, the destructive and reproductive energy associated with Shiva*

## Learning about religion

❶ Imagine that you are a Hindu. Write out a statement that describes what it means to be a member of your religion.

❷ Describe the three main Hindu denominations and explain the differences between them.

❸ Explain why you think some Hindus might choose to worship a variety of different deities rather than focus on just one deity.

## Learning from religion

❶ Conduct a class survey to find out the characteristics, features and functions people might associate with God and why. Produce a poster of your findings.

❷ Make up a statement explaining what it might mean to be religious.

❸ Explain who the most important people in your life are and why.

# ISKCON

## ISKCON

There are several **Vaishnava** groups in the UK. Many Vaishnavas belong to the International Society for Krishna Consciousness (ISKCON). The organization was founded in 1966 in New York by A. C. Bhaktivedanta Swami Prabhupada. ISKCON is based on the teachings of two Hindu **sacred** writings called the **Bhagavad Gita** and the **Bhagavad Purana**. It was set up to spread the message of **Sanatan Dharma** throughout the world. 'Krishna consciousness' is the idea of people being aware of God and their relationship with God in everything they do. Krishna is one of the **Sanskrit** names for God. It means the 'All-attractive One'.

A. C. Bhaktivedanta Swami Prabhupada, the founder of ISKCON

ISKCON offers people the opportunity to find out about Hinduism and to practise the Hindu faith. It also encourages people to live a simple and natural way of life.

ISKCON has established **mandirs**, or temples, in most major cities. These are centres of worship, missionary work, spiritual learning and retreat. Some mandirs also have farming communities attached to them. Many members of ISKCON worship at their local mandir, or temple, and practise Krishna consciousness at home with their families. Other **devotees**, or followers, have chosen to live as part of a religious community.

Bhaktivedanta Manor in Hertfordshire is the largest ISKCON centre in Europe. It stands in 70 acres of grounds, donated by the late George Harrison. He wanted it to be a 'showplace for Krishna consciousness'.

A place where people could get a taste of the splendour of devotional service to the Supreme Lord.

From *Dark Horse – The Secret Life of George Harrison*

The manor is regarded as a holy place dedicated to the practice, teaching and spreading of Sanatan Dharma, or **Hinduism**. Bhaktivedanta Manor consists of a theological college, a mandir, a theatre, a farm and gardens. Thousands of Krishna devotees and Hindus from around the London area visit it regularly to worship, celebrate festivals and learn more about their faith. Some Hindus choose to hold significant religious ceremonies there. Many people, particularly school children who are not Hindus, also visit the Manor to learn about Hinduism.

Bhaktivedanta Manor is a God-centred community, which enables people from all walks of life to find refuge, a sense of belonging, fellowship, spiritual fulfillment and meaning through living the simple precepts of Krishna consciousness as taught by His Divine Grace A. C. Bhaktivedanta Swami Prabhupada.

www.iskcon.org.uk/manor/aboutus.htlm

ISKCON is also known as the Hare Krishna Movement. This name comes from a **mantra** which devotees chant regularly, either in private or public, as part of their worship.

Hare Krishna, Hare Krishna, Krishna Krishna, Hare Hare, Hare Rama, Hare Rama, Rama Rama, Hare Hare.

Hindus believe that this chant contains God's holy names. They believe that by saying it they purify themselves and become closer to God.

## Learning about religion

❶ Research and produce an information leaflet about Bhaktivedanta Manor, which sets out its aims and describes what a visitor might find there. Use the Internet to do your research: www.iskcon.org.uk/manor

❷ Explain how you think visiting religious centres and places of worship can help people to learn about different religions.

❸ Discuss in pairs why you think showing hospitality to visitors might be an important part of Sanatan Dharma.

## Learning from religion

❶ Imagine that you are a teacher planning a visit to a place of worship. Write out a code of conduct for pupils to follow and prepare a worksheet for them to use.

❷ Design your own religious centre and place of worship, and explain its features.

❸ Explain what you would use 70 acres of land for and why?

# Sacred writings

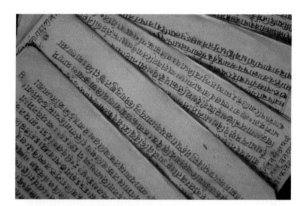

*Hindu scriptures written in Sanskrit*

## What are the Hindu sacred writings?

There are hundreds of **sacred** writings in **Hinduism**, but today many of these writings are not used. Most Hindu scriptures were originally written in **Sanskrit**, an ancient language.

Sanskrit is rarely used as an everyday language now. It is reserved for religious purposes only, although the special script in which it is written is used in many of the languages spoken in India today – including Hindi, the national language. Unless they are preparing to take up a position of religious responsibility, most Hindus do not learn or understand Sanskrit. They rely upon priests to read and translate the language during services. Some Hindu sacred writings have now been translated into English and other languages, such as Hindi and Gujurati. The Bhaktivedanta Book Trust (BBT), part of the International Society for Krishna Consciousness (ISKCON), is the world's largest publisher and distributor of books on Indian philosophy and the Hindu religion.

Each **denomination** in Hinduism has its own scriptures. Many of the sacred writings mentioned in this chapter all belong to **Vaishnavism**. This means that they are used by **devotees** of Vishnu and his **avatars**, such as Krishna or Rama. Other sacred writings also exist, some of which are used by **Shaivas**, devotees of Shiva. Many are written in another ancient language called Tamil.

## The oral tradition

Like other religions, Hinduism has an oral tradition of scripture. This means that the content of sacred texts was passed on by word of mouth for centuries, before eventually being written down. One reason for this was that in ancient times not many people could read and write and most ordinary Hindus learned about their faith by listening to the spoken word.

## Shruti and smriti

The sacred writings of Hinduism are divided into two main categories: **shruti** and **smriti**.

Shruti means 'that which is heard' and refers to writings that are believed to have been composed by God. They are thought to contain an accurate and true record of the words God spoke to ancient sages, wise and holy men. The sages remembered the words exactly as God spoke them, and passed them on accurately, word for word. Another term for shruti is 'revealed scriptures'. They are called this because Hindus believe that they are one way in which God has revealed Himself, or made Himself known, to human beings. The contents of these writings have remained the same for thousands of years. This is because Hindus believe that the words of God must not be altered or changed in any way.

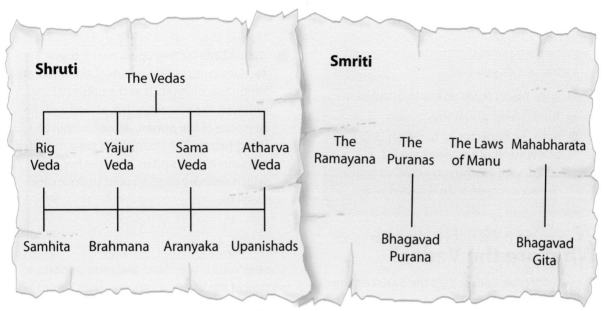

*Shruti and smriti, the two main categories of Hindu scriptures*

Smriti means 'that which has been remembered' and refers to writings that are believed to have been composed by realized souls (souls who are believed to have achieved **moksha**). These holy books are important to Hindus, but Hindus have different opinions about whether they are as important as the shruti writings, because they consist of what people can remember being told about God rather than the actual words of God. The contents of the smriti writings have changed over time and continue to be adapted to make them relevant to Hindus today.

Most Hindus do not seem to mind that the contents have changed. They say that the purpose of smriti writings is to help them to understand and experience God. It does not matter, therefore, if some of the details in the smriti writings change, as long as the meaning remains the same.

## Learning about religion

❶ Explain the difference between shruti and smriti scriptures in Hinduism, and describe Hindu attitudes towards them.

❷ Using the Internet, research the sacred writings of other religions. Compare your findings with Hinduism.

❸ 'You cannot rely on hearsay when talking and writing about God.' Do you agree? Give reasons for your answer.

## Learning from religion

❶ Describe your best memory of a pleasant event and explain why it is important to you.

❷ Discuss in groups the stories you can remember being told as children.

❸ Write a story that could teach people about the right or wrong way to behave in a certain situation.

# Shruti – the Vedas

In this section you will:

● learn what the Vedas contain and how Hindus use them today

● have the opportunity to reflect upon and write about some of the issues raised, such as who you would most like to have a conversation with and why.

## What are the Vedas?

The word '**Vedas**' comes from the **Sanskrit** word 'vid', meaning 'to know'. The Vedas are a collection of **sacred** writings which are believed to contain **shruti**, 'divinely given' or revealed knowledge. Collectively, the Vedas are sometimes referred to as Vedic literature. The period of literature in which they are believed to have been composed is called the Vedic period.

## What do the Vedas contain?

The Vedas are arranged under four headings: Rig Veda, Yajur Veda, Sama Veda and Atharva Veda. Each of the Vedas also has four parts.

1 Samhitas ('**mantras**'): these sections contain **prayers** and hymns, also known as mantras, written in an ancient form of Sanskrit.

2 Brahmanas ('belonging to the **Brahmins**', priests): these sections analyze and interpret the mantras contained in the Samhitas. They also provide information about where some religious rituals came from, and explain the meaning of certain ceremonies and the importance of saying prayers.

3 Aranyakas ('forest books'): these sections contain treatises, special essays, on **meditation** and **asceticism**. They were written for people such as **hermits** and **saints** who, for religious reasons, had chosen to live simple, isolated lives in forests.

4 Upanishads ('sitting down near'): these sections contain discussions about important Hindu teachings such as the origins of the universe, the characteristics of God and the presence of the **atman**, or soul, within all living beings. The Upanishads are a record of religious conversations between holy men, which ordinary people could sit down and listen to.

### The Rig Veda

The Rig Veda is the oldest and most important section of the Vedas. It contains 1028 hymns of praise, which are usually addressed to individual deities such as Agni, the deity of fire, or Varuna, the deity of the sky. The following is an example of a hymn from the Rig Veda.

*A hymn to Usha, the deity of the dawn*

In all ages has the deity Dawn shone, and shows her light today, endowed with riches.
So will she shine on coming days: immortal and undecaying, she moves on in her own strength.
In the sky's borders has she shone splendour: the deity has cast of the veil of darkness.
Dawn approaches in her magnificent chariot, awakening the world with purple horses.

The Rig Veda

The Rig Veda also mentions 33 **deities**, a list that has grown over time into thousands. However, it also contains a verse suggesting that from the very beginning of **Hinduism** some followers thought that all of the various deities were forms of the one God.

It is called Indra, Mitra, Varuna and Agni
And also Gautman the lovely-winged in heaven.
The real is one, though known by different names:
It is now called Agni, now Yama, now Matarishvan.

The Rig Veda

*A Brahmin priest reading excerpts from the Vedas at Varanasi, a holy city on the banks of the River **Ganga***

## How do Hindus use the Vedas?

Although **Sanatan Dharma** was originally based upon the teachings of the four Vedas, many modern Hindus do not read these sacred texts. Most Hindu **mandirs**, or temples, contain copies of the Vedas, but the book itself is not really used during worship. Even though the majority of hymns, prayers and readings are taken from the Vedas, the priest may read or chant selected passages from a smaller book, which contains excerpts from the Vedas, or he might follow the ancient oral tradition and recite them from memory. Listening to Sanskrit, the sacred language of their religion, is an important part of worship for Hindus.

The Vedas are important to Hindus because they are believed to contain the word of God. They are the oldest and most sacred of all the Hindu scriptures upon which **Hinduism** was founded.

### Learning about religion

❶ Write a paragraph explaining what the Vedas are and what they contain.

❷ In pairs, role-play two Hindus discussing the importance of the Vedas and the influence they have on their lives.

❸ Describe how the Vedas might be used during Hindu worship.

### Learning from religion

❶ Explain why you think some people might choose, for religious reasons, to live on their own in a forest.

❷ Who would you most like to 'sit down near' and have a conversation with?

❸ Write a poem about the dawn.

# *Smriti*

In this section you will:

● learn about other sacred writings that Hindus use

● have the opportunity to reflect upon and write about some of the issues raised, such as the value of keeping promises.

## What other sacred writings do Hindus use?

The remainder of the **sacred** writings that most modern Hindus use are called **smriti**, 'that which has been remembered'. This means that they have been composed by realized souls, souls who are believed to have achieved **moksha**.

## The Puranas

The **Puranas** are a group of smriti texts. The word 'purana' means 'ancient'. These writings are called this because they contain stories and legends that are set in the very distant past, or even before the world began. The Puranas focus on the main Hindu **deities**, Vishnu, Shiva and Brahma. They also teach about religion and morality. The twelve books of the **Bhagavad Purana** are about the incarnations of Vishnu and the famous stories of Krishna as a child, who plays tricks on his parents.

The oldest Purana is thought to have been written about 300 CE, with the rest being put into writing over the following 1000 years, which is known as the Puranic age. This group of texts shows how the Hindu religion has developed from the time the **Vedas** were written. They are significant for Hindus because much of modern **Hinduism** is based upon them.

*Krishna as a child, stealing milk from the butterchurn*

## The Laws of Manu

The **Laws of Manu** are a collection of smriti law books that contain rules about how Hindus should live their lives. The word 'manu' means 'man'. According to Hindu mythology, there are fourteen Manus. They are the ancestors of human beings, each of whom ruled over the earth for a period of time. The Laws of Manu are important for Hindus today, although recently some of these laws regarding the treatment of women and certain social groups, or **varnas**, have been criticized and questioned because they are said to promote inequality.

# The Mahabharata and the Bhagavad Gita

The **Mahabharata** is another smriti text. The word 'Mahabharata' comes from the **Sanskrit** words 'Bharat' (meaning India) and 'maha' (meaning great). Another name for this book is the Great Indian Epic. An epic is a long poem that tells the story of a legendary hero or heroine. The Mahabharata is the world's longest poem – it has about 3 million words, 220 thousand lines and 100 thousand verses!

The poem tells the story of the exploits of two royal families, who trick and fight each other to see who should be the rightful ruler of a country. One of the central characters is Krishna, who acts as the charioteer for one of the warring cousins, Prince Arjuna, in the Battle of Kurukshetra. The conversation between Krishna and Arjuna before the battle is known as the **Bhagavad Gita**. It is the most popular of all the Hindu sacred writings. Its name comes from the Sanskrit words 'gita' (meaning song) and 'bhagavad', a name for God. Another name for this book is 'The Song of God'.

The Mahabharata and the Bhagavad Gita are significant for Hindus because they explain, in story form, important Hindu beliefs and ideas which are expressed in the **Vedas**, for example, **samsara**. Reading and listening to these poems helps Hindus to understand how God expects them to behave.

# The Ramayana

The **Ramayana** takes the form of an epic, although the poem is much shorter than the Mahabharata. The Ramayana focuses on the idea of **dharma**, or religious duty. It explores the triumph of good over evil, which Hindus see more in terms of the victory of knowledge and wisdom over foolishness and ignorance. This epic stresses the importance of behaving in a **moral** way, and emphasizes the value of courage, loyalty, fidelity and keeping your word.

It puts forward a positive view of Hindu women by pointing out their inner strength and showing the sacrifices they are capable of making. The word 'Ramayana' means the 'inner journey of Rama' and the poem focuses on the exploits of Rama, the seventh **avatar** of Vishnu, and his companions. Rama is accompanied by his wife, Sita, his brother, Laksmana, and Hanuman, the monkey deity. The poem was probably written sometime between 500 BCE and 200 CE. The story is retold every year at **Divali** and is remembered during the festival of Dassehra.

## Learning about religion

❶ List the main smriti texts and explain briefly what each one contains.

❷ Describe which smriti text you would most like to read and explain why.

❸ Research the Ramayana, and explain which parts of the story you think best illustrate the value of courage, loyalty, fidelity and keeping your word. Use the Internet to look for information.

## Learning from religion

❶ Make up your own set of laws which, if followed, would enable a community to live in peace and harmony.

❷ Write a poem about good versus evil.

❸ 'You should always keep your promises.' Do you agree with this statement? Give reasons for your answer.

# The Trimurti 1

In this section you will:

- learn what Hindus believe to be true about God

- find out how they understand and represent God

- have the opportunity to reflect upon some of the issues raised, such as the different roles people perform in the course of their everyday lives

- be able to think about why people might find it difficult to agree with some of the things Hindus say about God.

**G**: generator – this represents God's ability to create things

**O**: operator – this represents God's ability to preserve things and keep them going

**D**: destroyer – this represents God's ability to destroy things

Hindus believe that these roles are fulfilled by the three deities of the Trimurti, who work together to maintain the continuous cycle of life within the universe.

## How do Hindus understand God?

Many Hindus believe in One Supreme God, whom they call Brahman, but they worship that one God in various forms, according to the different functions they believe He performs. Hindus believe that God is omnipresent, always present everywhere and in all livings things. They also believe that God may be represented in masculine and feminine ways. A unique feature of **Hinduism** is that God is worshipped in male and female forms. It teaches that both men and women are 'different wings of the same bird' (**Swami** Vivekananda). The feminine aspect of God, also known as the Mother Goddess, is represented through the various female **deities** of Hinduism. Some Hindus believe that there are as many as 33 million deities, each of which have a special role to perform within the universe.

The three main deities in Hinduism, known as the **Trimurti**, are Brahma, the creator, Vishnu, the preserver, and Shiva, the destroyer. The word Trimurti means 'three forms'. Some Hindus say that the three letters of the word GOD relate to the three main functions of God.

## How do Hindus represent God?

*The Trimurti is sometimes depicted as a three-headed man. This symbolizes the Hindu belief that Brahma, Vishnu and Shiva are all aspects of One Supreme Being, Brahman. Modern Hindus do not normally worship the Trimurti as a deity. They prefer to concentrate on individual aspects of God instead.*

One way Hindus represent God is by producing visual images of the deities, either in the form of statues, also known as **murtis**, or in the form of pictures. The images Hindus use today have evolved over time and are the result of the ideas and visions of **saints**, sages and mystics throughout the ages. These symbolic representations of God often have superhuman features and may carry certain objects that signify important Hindu ideas about the nature of God.

# Brahma

Hinduism teaches that Brahma is the creator of the universe. All living beings are said to have evolved from him. Brahma is also believed to be responsible for the four **Vedas**, the most important Hindu sacred writings, which are said to have come from his head.

Traditionally, Brahma is shown with four heads, bearded faces and four arms. His four heads enable him to look in every direction at once and represent the Hindu belief that God is omniscient, or all-knowing. His four arms represent the Hindu belief that God is omnipotent, or all-powerful.

Brahma holds a variety of symbolic objects. He is usually shown carrying a bowl or water jug, which symbolizes his role as creator, because water is important to life. He may also have a sacrificial ladle or spoon, which acts as his sceptre and is a reminder of both his **divine** status and the importance of offerings during worship. And he may have a string of beads, called a **mala**, and a book, which represents the Vedas.

Brahma is sometimes depicted sitting on a **lotus** flower, a symbol of purity, and accompanied by a white swan, which acts as his vehicle.

Although Brahma is an important member of the Trimurti, he is not worshipped as widely as the other two members, Vishnu and Shiva. One reason given for this is that, as creator, his work for the time being is complete.

*Brahma, the creator of the universe*

## Learning about religion

❶ 'God is one and many.' Explain how a Hindu might respond to this statement.

❷ Write a job description for each member of the Trimurti.

❸ Describe and explain how Hindus represent God. Use illustrations to support your statements.

## Learning from religion

❶ Describe your three main roles and evaluate whether they complement or contradict each other.

❷ Explain why some people might find it difficult to believe that God is omnipresent, omniscient and omnipotent.

❸ What job would you most like to do and why?

## Vishnu

**Hinduism** teaches that Vishnu is the preserver of the universe. He is said to protect the world from evil, and represents mercy and goodness. Vishnu is believed to have come to earth in nine different forms, known as **avatars**, or incarnations. His most celebrated avatars are those of Rama and Krishna.

*Vishnu, a member of the Trimurti, is believed to be responsible for preserving the universe*

Vishnu is shown as blue or dark blue because Hindus believe he is like the sky, everywhere and everlasting. He has three vertical lines on his forehead to symbolize that he is member of the **Trimurti**. In two of his hands he holds a discus and a mace, which are his magic weapons. Vishnu's other hands contain a white conch shell and a **lotus** flower, a symbol of purity. In ancient times the conch shell was blown to signify the beginning and end of battles. It was also blown by warriors to announce their victory. Some Hindus believe that the sound of the conch shell is capable of keeping away evil spirits and saving human beings from disaster.

Vishnu is sometimes depicted sitting on a large serpent. Some Hindus believe that snakes are **sacred** creatures and they are the subject of many myths and legends. Traditionally, the snake has been feared and worshipped by some Hindus, in the hope that the snake will protect its devotees.

Vishnu's vehicle is Garuda, the king of the birds, a half-man, half-eagle.

## Shiva

Hinduism teaches that Shiva is the **deity** of destruction and a reproductive power. This is because by destroying things he also makes renewal and new growth possible. His energy, Shakti, is capable of both destroying and reproducing things. Shakti is believed to take the female form as Shiva's consort Parvati, and as other deities such as Durga and Kali.

Shiva is also known by many names and is shown in different ways. In one of his most well-known forms he is depicted as an ascetic (someone who chooses to lead a harsh and simple life), usually sitting cross-legged on a tiger skin, deep in **meditation**. The tiger skin is a symbol of Shiva's bravery and his ability to overcome his enemies.

*Another popular image of Shiva is 'Shiva Nataraja', the 'Lord of the Dance'. He is shown dancing in a circle of flames and standing on the dwarf of evil and ignorance. The flames symbolize **Shakti**, energy. They also remind Hindus of the fires of **cremation**, which follow death*

Shiva is shown wearing a simple loin cloth. He has a crescent moon in his long matted hair and a top knot out of which comes the **Ganga**, the Hindus' most sacred river. Snakes are also entwined in his hair and act as armlets and bracelets.

Shiva has three horizontal lines on his forehead to show that he is a member of the Trimurti. His throat is blue, which is said to be the result of drinking poison from the ocean in order to save the world from destruction. He has three eyes and is understood to be able to see the past, the present and the future. The third eye in the middle of his forehead is always closed and is believed only to open in anger, when the light from it is capable of destroying anyone who does evil. He holds a trident, a three-pronged spear, which represents the Trimurti.

One of his other hands is usually empty and raised, palm outwards, as a symbol of protection and blessing for those who worship him (see page 5).

Shiva's vehicle is Nandi, a white bull. The bull is a symbol of fertility. Statues of bulls are often found in shrines dedicated to Shiva.

## Learning about religion

**1** Produce a poster that shows and explains the main symbols associated with the Trimurti.

**2** Research the other avatars of Vishnu and record your findings in the form of a table. You could use the Internet to help you.

**3** In groups of three, role-play Brahma, Vishnu and Shiva discussing their roles and how they work together to maintain the cycle of life within the universe.

## Learning from religion

**1** Describe your three most precious possessions and explain why they are important to you. What could they tell people about your character?

**2** In groups, provide examples of how destruction has made new beginnings possible.

**3** Discuss in pairs how you think the cycle of life within the universe is maintained.

# Deities 1

In this section you will:

● learn about some of the other Hindu deities

● have the opportunity to explore some of the issues raised, such as how positive role models might influence people's behaviour

## Rama

Rama is the seventh **avatar** of Vishnu. Hindus believe that Rama came to earth with his companions in order to defeat a wicked demon and to show what an ideal human being should be like. His story is told in the **Ramayana**, one of the Hindu **sacred** scriptures.

Rama is shown as a human being with blue skin and marks on his forehead like Vishnu. He carries a bow and has a quiver full of arrows on his back.

## Krishna

Although Krishna is described as the eighth avatar of Vishnu, some Hindus believe that he is the Avatari, the source of all the other avatars, hence the terms 'Krishna' and 'Vishnu' are often used to mean the same thing. Krishna is a very popular Hindu **deity** and, like Rama, is shown in human form with blue skin and marks on his forehead, like Vishnu. Krishna also carries a flute and wears a peacock feather in his hair. He is sometimes shown with a white cow. This reminds Hindus of one of the many stories about him when he flirted with the gopis, or cow girls.

*Rama, his wife Sita and companions. The story of the Ramayana is remembered during the festivals of **Divali** and Dassehra*

*Lakshmi is worshipped during the festival of Divali*

# Lakshmi

Lakshmi is the consort of Vishnu. Hindus believe that she is the representation of his female energy, and the deity of happiness, wealth and good fortune. Every time Vishnu has come to earth as an **avatar**, Lakshmi, in various forms, is said to have come too. Lakshmi is usually shown either sitting or standing on a **lotus** flower with elephants on either side of her. Gold coins fall from one of her hands and symbolize her ability to reward **devotees** with prosperity.

# Parvati

Parvati is Shiva's consort. She, along with all the other female deities within **Hinduism**, is understood to represent the feminine aspect of God. Hindus believe that Parvati is a form of **Shakti**, the destructive and reproductive energy associated with Shiva. Shiva and Parvati are often shown together and, like other deities, they symbolize the male and female aspects of the One Supreme Being. Shiva and Parvati are also the parents of Ganesha, the elephant-headed deity.

As Parvati, the Mother Goddess, Shakti is gentle, peace-loving and family orientated, but she can take other more fearsome forms, such as Durga or Kali (see pages 5 and 21). Traditionally, Parvati is worshipped by married Hindu women in the hope of a happy married life.

*Parvati holding Ganesha*

## Learning about religion

1. Research Hanuman, the monkey deity, and present your findings in the form of an educational poster. You could use the Internet to help you.

2. Write an article about Krishna for an ISKCON publication.

3. Explain why you think young Hindu women might see Parvati as a positive role model.

## Learning from religion

1. 'A friend in need is a friend indeed.' Explain what this statement means and say whether or not you agree with it, giving reasons for your answer.

2. Describe what you think the 'ideal human being' would be like in terms of his or her characteristics and behaviour.

3. Identify someone who you think could be a positive role model for young people and explain your choice.

# Deities 2

In this section you will:
● learn more about the different Hindu deities
● have the opportunity to explore some of the issues raised, such as how people overcome difficulties in life.

## Durga

Durga is another fierce and powerful form of **Shakti**. She too is believed to manifest the destructive, reproductive energy of Shiva and looks ferocious. Durga rides on a lion and carries a variety of objects, several of which are weapons, in her eight hands. One Hindu story says that she was given her great strength and weaponry by the **deities** that needed her help to defeat a cunning buffalo demon.

*Durga is worshipped during the festival of Navaratri*

*Saraswati is usually worshipped during the festival of Vasanta Panchami, also known as Saraswati **puja**. The festival marks the beginning of spring*

## Saraswati

Saraswati is the consort of Brahma. She is the deity of learning and the arts. Saraswati is described as being very beautiful, and is depicted as having pale skin and fine clothes. She has four arms, which represent four aspects of the human personality: mind, intellect, ego and conscience. Saraswati is often shown carrying a stringed musical instrument, a copy of the **Vedas** and a **mala**. She is usually accompanied by a white swan, the vehicle of Brahma, and a peacock.

# Ganesha

Ganesha is the son of Parvati and Shiva. He is the deity of wisdom and good fortune, and is also known as the 'remover of obstacles'. Traditionally, Ganesha is the first deity prayed to during worship to ensure good luck and success. All religious ceremonies and many non-religious activities begin with a **prayer** to him. He also appears on greetings cards that announce happy events such as a birth or a wedding.

Ganesha is shown as a short, pot-bellied man with an elephant's head. His large stomach represents prosperity, as does the dish of sweetmeats that he holds in one of his four hands. Like Shiva, one of his other hands is raised with his palm facing outwards, which signifies a blessing for his devotees. Ganesha might also hold a lotus flower and an axe, which represent his purity and his ability to remove obstacles. He is accompanied by a black rat,

which symbolizes that all creatures great and small are of value and have a purpose in life.

# Kali

The Shakti energy of Shiva also finds form in Kali, a fierce and very powerful form of Parvati. She looks frightening and represents the awesome power of Mother Nature, which should be admired, respected and dreaded. Kali wears a necklace of skulls and severed arms hang from her waist. She might also hold a severed head and a sickle, a deadly weapon, in two of her four hands. Kali rides on the corpse of a demon whom she has destroyed (see page 5).

*The Hindu festival of Ganesh-Chaturthi celebrates Ganesha's birthday*

## Learning about religion

1. Draw a diagram showing the relationships between the deities mentioned on pages 14–21.

2. Do further research on one of the deities discussed and prepare a booklet on your findings. You could use the Internet to help you.

3. Compare and contrast Hindu ideas about God with those of two other religions you have studied. Produce a chart showing the differences and similarities.

## Learning from religion

1. Describe your favourite animal and explain your choice.

2. Design your own range of symbols to represent power, learning, prosperity, good luck and success.

3. Discuss in pairs what qualities you think a person needs in order to overcome difficulties in life.

# Teachers and leaders

In this section you will:

● learn about some of the teachers and leaders in Hinduism

● have the opportunity to discuss and write about some of the issues raised, such as the role of stories and the different forms education can take.

*Hindus listening to a story from scripture. The storyteller often knows large portions of scripture by heart, and will adapt stories to suit their audience*

## The mandir priest

Every **mandir**, or temple, has its own priest or priests. Many priests are well educated and have undergone extensive mental, spiritual and physical training in order to carry out their duties. The ability to discipline the mind and senses is considered important in **Hinduism**. Priests have detailed knowledge of Hindu scriptures, and the teachings and practices of **Sanatan Dharma**.

Two of the most important functions of a Hindu priest are conducting religious ceremonies and caring for the **shrines** in the mandir. This includes washing and dressing the various **murtis** as an act of devotional service to God.

Hinduism teaches that priests must purify themselves internally and externally before worship can take place. External purity can be achieved by washing or bathing, ideally in a **sacred** river or pool. Internal purity may be gained by following rules about a vegetarian diet, and not drinking alcohol, by following a celibate lifestyle, and studying the Hindu sacred writings, meditating or practising yoga.

## The storyteller

Storytelling is a very important tradition in Hinduism. Many Hindus learn about their faith and what is expected of them is by listening to stories about the **deities**. They may hear the same stories over and over again, but they never

get tired or bored with them. This is because the stories can be understood on many levels and can help Hindus to make sense of life.

## The guru

A **guru** is a spiritual teacher. Hindus believe that certain people have developed their spirituality to the point where they can teach others about God and help them to live according to their **dharma**. Some disciples spend years with their spiritual teacher. Others may meet them once in a lifetime or never actually see them at all, in which case the only contact is through written material or pictures of the guru. Many Hindu shrines contain pictures of gurus, and **devotees** honour and respect them in the same way they would a deity. This is because the guru is considered to be a representative of God and has the power to help their disciple to reach **moksh**, liberation from **samsara**.

### Sathya Sai Baba

Sathya Sai Baba is a very popular modern guru. He is thought to have as many as 15 million followers throughout the world, many of whom consider him to be an **avatar** of God. Thousands of his disciples wait daily at his **ashram** in India

*Sathya Sai Baba announced his mission in 1940. Every day, for more than 50 years, he has walked among and talked to pilgrims who come to see him*

in the hope of seeing him. An ashram is a place set up to encourage spiritual development. Sai Baba emphasizes the importance of all religions and the need for religious unity if the world is to know peace.

There is only one religion, the religion of love. There is only one language, the language of the heart. There is only one race, the race of humanity. There is only one God, and He is omnipresent.

Sathya Sai Baba

*The Universal Symbol of the Unity of Religions, the symbol of the Sathya Sai Service Organization*

## Learning about religion

❶ Describe the roles of the priest, storyteller and guru. Explain how each of these individuals might feature in a Hindu's life.

❷ Study carefully the quote from Sathya Sai Baba. Explain what you think he is saying about religion and God.

❸ Produce a poster that promotes the idea of unity between religions.

## Learning from religion

❶ 'Stories are for children.' Do you agree? Give reasons for your answer.

❷ 'There is more to education than what you learn in school.' Discuss.

❸ List reasons why people might not be tolerant of each other and suggest ways to overcome intolerance.

23

# What do Hindus believe?

In this section you will:

- learn about some important Hindu beliefs
- have the opportunity to reflect upon and write about some of the issues raised, such as the possible benefits of meditation and yoga.

**Hinduism** is a very diverse religious tradition. This means that there is a wide range of beliefs within the religion. Nevertheless, there is a set of basic beliefs that most Hindus share and that gives **Sanatan Dharma** its distinctive identity.

Hindus believe in One Supreme God, whom they call Brahman. Hindus believe that God is omnipotent, omniscient, omnipresent and eternal.

Hindus believe that all matter is **maya** (illusory). They describe it as this because even though physical objects such as the body appear to be permanent and real, they do not last forever. Hindus believe that only the **atman**, or soul, endures. They say that becoming to attached to material things is a cause of suffering. This is because material things are finite which means that one day they will cease to exist or be important.

## Samsara

Hindus believe in **transmigration**. This is the belief that the atman survives after death whereupon it enters a new body. This continuous cycle of birth, death and rebirth is called **samsara**, also known as **reincarnation**. Samsara might involve the atman experiencing numerous lives as a variety of different species. The aim of all Hindus is to live their lives in such a way that their atman can be liberated from transmigration and reach a condition known as **moksha**. Moksha is when the atman is free from samsara and is united with God.

## Karma

Hindus believe in **karma**. This is also known as the 'law of cause and effect', which states that all thoughts and actions have results that correspond to them. Hindus believe that ultimately every person will bear the consequences of his or her own deeds, either in this life or the next. If they behave well and live according to their **dharma**, their next life will better than the one they have now. The reverse is also true: if they behave badly and do not live according to their dharma, their next life will be worse than the one they have now.

Agami karma: *all the echoes performed in this life will affect the future. Good actions can help reduce suffering. Bad actions can increase suffering*

*A **Brahmin** practising yoga*

# Spiritual development

Hindus believe that following the advice and teachings of a **guru**, or spiritual teacher, is important for their spiritual development. They also recognize that they need to worship God regularly, both in a **mandir** and at home, and participate in other religious rituals throughout the course of their lives.

Another thing Hindus are committed to is the idea of obtaining internal and external purity through practices such as bathing in **sacred** water, following a strict diet, which includes not drinking alcohol, **meditation** and yoga. The fulfilling of one's religious duties, dharma, without looking for or expecting personal reward is thought to bring a person nearer to moksha.

Hindus believe that the greatest dharma is to practise **ahimsa**. Ahimsa means 'not killing' or 'non-violence'. It involves having reverence and respect for all life. Many Hindus are vegetarians because of this belief. They do not eat meat, fish and eggs because they think that once animals and other creatures are brought into this world they should be allowed to develop and live out their natural life span and not be killed for food.

## Learning about religion

❶ Produce a glossary of key terms used in this section.

❷ Discuss in groups how some Hindu beliefs mentioned on these pages could affect the life of a believer. Report back to the rest of your class using examples to support your statements.

❸ Under separate headings, summarize the Hindu beliefs mentioned on these pages. Explain what you think about the ideas discussed.

## Learning from religion

❶ 'Things are only real if you can see them.' Do you agree with this statement? Explain your reasons and give examples to support your statements.

❷ 'Meditation is to the mind what water is to the body.' Explain what you think this statement means.

❸ Research the different forms of yoga that are practised around the world. Compare and contrast religious and non-religious interpretations of yoga. You could use the Internet to look for infomation.

# Society

In this section you will:

● learn about how Hindu society has been organized

● have the opportunity to reflect upon and discuss some of the issues raised, such as the significance of your occupation and employment.

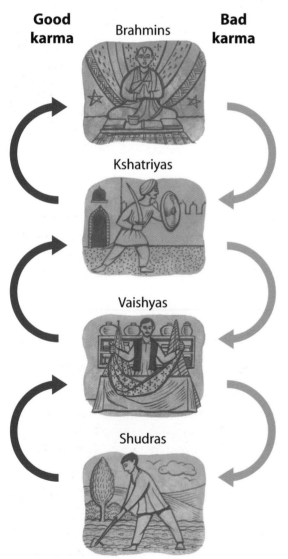

**Good karma**   Brahmins   **Bad karma**

Kshatriyas

Vaishyas

Shudras

*The four varnas*

## How is Hindu society organized?

Traditionally, Indian society has been divided into four main classes called **varnas**. Each of the four varnas, or groups, is associated with a particular occupation and has a status attached to it. The higher the varna, the purer, or closer to God and **moksha**, people were thought to be.

**Brahmins**, who were priests and advisors, were the first and most important varna. The second varna were the **Kshatriyas**, soldiers and rulers. Next came the **Vaishyas**, shopkeepers, traders and farmers, followed by the **Shudras**, unskilled workers and those who sought employment. Over time, these four divisions have developed into a complex social system with each varna being further divided into thousands of sub-groups called **jatis**, or **castes**. A jati is made up of numerous families who follow the same occupation. This way of organizing society is known as the **caste system**.

A fifth group of people emerged, made up of people who did not belong to any of the four main varnas and who were outside the caste system. These people were called 'untouchables'. They did the dirtiest and most unpleasant jobs, and were forbidden from worshipping or mixing with people from other castes.

Many Hindus believe that the jati or caste you are born into depends upon the **karma** you have accumulated in previous lives. In **Sanskrit** the word 'jati' means 'birth'. The idea that the combined consequences of your thoughts and actions are carried over from one life to the next is called **samchita karma**. If the karma built up is good, then the **atman** will be reborn a stage closer to moksha, into a higher position in life. If the karma built up is bad, the atman will be reborn a stage further away from moksha.

*Members of an unskilled jati decorating pots in India*

According to Hindu scriptures, the varnas are religious divisions and came into being supernaturally. In one Hindu creation story, the four varnas originated from Purusha, the first man. The Brahmins came from his mouth or head, the Kshatriyas from his arms, the Vaishyas from his thighs, and the Shudras from his feet.

In the past, Hindus could only associate with members of their own jati. Nowadays, although these divisions still exist, there is some flexibility and movement between the different castes and varnas.

## Learning about religion

❶ Explain how Indian society is organized. Describe the possible effects of this structure on the everyday life of a Hindu.

❷ Why are the divisions in Indian society believed to exist?

❸ Research the life and work of Mahatma Ghandi and evaluate the contribution he made to Indian society.

## Learning from religion

❶ Do you think that your occupation and status in this life is determined by your behaviour in a previous lifetime? Give reasons for your answer.

❷ 'It does not matter what job you do as long as you earn your living honestly.' Discuss this statement in pairs.

❸ Explain why it might be easy or difficult for some people to follow the same occupation as other members of their family.

# Symbols 1

One of the main ways in which Hindus use symbolism is to express their ideas, feelings and beliefs about God. All of the **deities** within **Hinduism** are symbolic representations of God, according to the different functions He is believed to perform. Each of the main deities is shown in a particular way. Many have supernatural features and specific items connected with them that represent qualities associated with God.

Another use of symbolism is in stories. Hindu **sacred** writings contain numerous tales that have important symbolic meanings.

Symbolism also affects the way Hindus worship, the actions they perform and the objects they use. It affects the way they look, the language they use and the way they describe God.

## Aum

Om is the Askara, or imperishable [lasting] syllable.
Om is the universe, and this is the exposition [explanation] of Om.
The past, the present and the future, all that was, all that is, all that will be, is Om.
Likewise all else that may exist beyond the bounds of time, that too is Om.

Mandukya Upanishad

*Aum: the imperishable syllable*

**Aum**, sometimes spelt Om, is the main symbol of Hinduism. It represents God and the sound of creation. Aum is a sacred sound for Hindus. They believe that it is the first sound God made and the basis of all other sounds in the universe, including speech. Aum is said in chants and **meditations** to achieve 'deep relaxation, comfort, blessing, peace and tranquility'.

## The swastika

*A rangoli pattern using the swastika, made for the festival of **Divali***

The word 'swastika' comes from Sanskrit and means 'well being'. In Hinduism, the symbol of the swastika represents good fortune. Hindus may draw it on the opening pages of account books, or on the floors of their houses during festivals or other important occasions. It is also used during marriage ceremonies and worship.

The four arms of the swastika are said to represent three things:

● space – the four directions (north, south, east and west)

● time – the four ashramas (stages in life)

● knowledge – the four Vedas.

The swastika has been used throughout history in positive and negative ways. It was adopted by Hitler and his Nazi party during World War II, and has become associated with the Third Reich.

## The coconut

The coconut has a number of symbolic meanings. One interpretation is that the three round dots found on the base of coconut represent the Trimurti, the three main forms of God. Another understanding is that these dots symbolize the belief that, in effect, human beings have three eyes – two physical eyes and a third inner, invisible eye, which can distinguish right from wrong and which acts as a conscience.

*The coconut is used frequently during religious ceremonies to signify purity, fertility and blessing*

# The lotus flower

*The lotus: a symbol of good overcoming evil*

The lotus represents purity and goodness. This is because the plant grows in muddy water, yet when the flowers open they are clean. Some of the deities are often shown carrying, sitting or standing on a lotus flower. This shows that they are not affected by the evil in the world.

## Learning about religion

❶ Draw a diagram showing the main ways in which Hindus use symbols.

❷ In groups, compare and contrast the Hindu use of symbolism with how symbols are used in two other religions.

❸ Evaluate the importance of symbolism for a Hindu in his or her religious life.

## Learning from religion

❶ Describe your favourite sound and explain why you like to hear it.

❷ Design your own symbol to represent the triumph of good over evil.

❸ Discuss in pairs how you use symbols in your everyday life.

# *Symbols 2*

In this section you will:

● learn about some more symbols Hindus use

● have the opportunity to explore some of the issues raised, such as the value of using symbols to express beliefs, feelings and ideas.

## Ash

Body markings are another way in which Hindus symbolize their beliefs. Some Hindus place ash on their foreheads or body to represent their belief that everything except the **atman** is **maya** (illusory) and will ultimately perish. Ash also signifies **cremation**. This reminds Hindus that life is short and that their **dharma** is to live life in a way that shows love and respect for all living things.

## Sindoora

The sindoora is a red mark placed in the parting of the hair of Hindu women who are married. It represents the power of the Mother Goddess, Shakta, the feminine aspect of God. Hindu women wear it in the hope that the Mother Goddess will protect their husbands and grant them long life.

## Bindi

Traditionally, the bindi is a red dot worn by married women between their eyebrows. It is a symbol of Parvati, the consort of Shiva, who is considered by Hindus to be the ideal wife. The bindi signifies the **Shakti** energy of Shiva in the female form, and represents his third eye. It is put on during worship, and is worn as a symbol of protection and blessing for women and their husbands. Today, bindis are often worn for personal decoration and have no religious significance for the people who wear them.

*Shaktas, **devotees** of the Mother Goddess, apply a round or slightly enlarged red mark on their foreheads*

*Hindus bathing in the Ganga at Varanasi, India*

# Water

Water is an important symbol in **Hinduism**. It is seen as a source of life because all living things need water to survive. A jar of water is sometimes placed on a pile of corn outside the houses of newly-wed couples to symbolize fertility, in the hope that they will be blessed with children.

Water is also used for cleansing and purification. Hindus wash or bathe before worship and at death the body is washed prior to cremation. Holy water is sometimes sprinkled on the ground to remove evil from a particular place.

In India, there are seven **sacred** rivers. The most sacred of these is the **Ganga**. The Ganga is the subject of numerous legends and is believed to have amazing properties. One feature is that the water from the Ganga does not appear to go stale even after being kept in a jar for several months. According to Hindu scriptures, anywhere the Ganga flows becomes sacred. Millions of **devotees** bathe in the river whenever they get the opportunity. They also take home water from the river in sealed jars, which they place in their household **shrines**.

## Learning about religion

❶ Produce an educational poster for use in a junior school that illustrates and explains the different symbols Hindus use in their religion.

❷ 'People only decorate their bodies because they are vain.' Explain how a Hindu might respond to this.

❸ In groups, research and prepare a report on how water is used as a symbol in the six major world religions.

## Learning from religion

❶ Design a series of body markings to represent four of your main beliefs. Explain your ideas.

❷ 'Symbols are just an excuse to draw patterns and pictures.' Do you agree with this statement? Give reasons.

# *Worship 1*

In this section you will:

● learn how Hindus worship in the home

● have the opportunity to discuss and write about some of the issues raised, such as the role of the family in religion and society.

## How do Hindus worship?

Worship is part of a Hindu's **dharma**. Hindus believe that God is omnipresent, in everything. This means that their everyday lives can be an act of worship and religious practices form part of their daily routine. **Hinduism**, or **Sanatan Dharma**, is not just a religion, it is a way of life.

There are also times when Hindus worship in specific ways at home and in **mandirs**, or temples. All forms of ritualistic worship in Hinduism are called **puja**. The regulations and rituals associated with puja are written down in the **Vedas**.

## Worship in the home

Many Hindus get up early, bathe and perform devotional activities such as **prayer**, **meditation**, reciting **mantras** and studying **sacred** writings. They will also take part in puja at least once a day, either in the morning or in the evening. In addition to this, Hindus participate in numerous other religious ceremonies, such as **samskars**, and celebrations, for example festivals, throughout the course of their lives.

All Hindu homes usually have a small **shrine**, which is used for family puja and which can sometimes take the form of a cupboard or shelf. It contains a **murti**, or image, of the family's chosen **deity**, and objects associated with them. It also has flowers, jewellery and other decorations, such as tinsel and small lights, to show that the deity is honoured and special. The murti represents God and is therefore treated

with great care and respect. This includes the murti being washed and groomed regularly. Murtis help worshippers to concentrate and focus their attention on God. Sometimes there are murtis and pictures of other deities and important leaders or **gurus** in the shrine too. One of these is usually Ganesha (the remover of obstacles), who is normally worshipped before all other deities.

A shrine also contains a variety of other items used during worship. These items reflect the fact that puja involves the five senses and makes symbolic references to the five elements of the universe: earth, air, fire, water and ether, from which Hindus believe everything was made. Many of these items might be placed on a puja tray.

In the home, puja is usually performed by the mother or wife of the family.

*A Hindu family shrine in the UK*

- A bell: this is rung at the beginning of puja to let the deity know that worship is about to start. Hindus believe that it is unreasonable to expect something so great as God to be waiting upon human beings all of the time.

- A dish containing sandalwood paste, vermilion or ashes: this is used to mark the worshipper's forehead as both a symbol of his or her devotion, and the blessing and protection of God.

- Offerings of food such as rice, nuts, sweets and fruit: these offerings are seen as symbolic exchanges of love between the worshipper and the deity.

*A puja tray*

- A pot containing holy water: this is used for cleansing and purification. Some shrines have a jar containing water from the **Ganga**, the River Ganges.

- An incense stick and holder: incense sticks are lit to purify and cleanse the air where prayers are being said and to create a holy atmosphere.

- An **arti** lamp with five wicks, each of which represents one of the five elements of the universe: earth, air, fire, water and ether. Hindus believe that fire can be used to communicate with God and transfer His blessings.

## Learning from religion

❶ Describe a tradition that you would like to keep in your family and explain why.

❷ Someone once said 'A family who prays together stays together.' Explain what you think that person meant and say whether you agree, giving reasons for your answer.

❸ Discuss in pairs what you think the main roles of a family are and how members of a family unit should behave towards each other. Produce a 'family charter', which sets out the main functions of a family and describes the rights and responsibilities of parents and children.

## Learning about religion

❶ Discuss in pairs why Hindus might choose to worship God.

❷ Imagine that you are a young Hindu. Write a diary account describing how and why you worship God at home.

❸ In groups, make a replica of a Hindu shrine and produce a guide to worship in the home that explains how each item is used.

## Worship in the mandir

The Hindu place of worship is called a **mandir**, or temple. Although almost every Hindu home contains a **shrine** for personal worship, the mandir has a special significance for Hindus. This is because **Hinduism** teaches that the mandir is the 'home of God'. Hindus believe that although God is in everything, He is personally present in the

mandir in the form of the **deities** that represent Him. Worshipping in the temple gives **devotees** the opportunity to relate to God directly.

There are thousands of purpose-built mandirs in India. Some of them are large and include several buildings. Others are very small and simple, and can take the form of a roadside shrine. In other countries, such as the UK, mandirs are mainly buildings that have been adapted. Depending upon its size, a mandir might contain several shrines. The largest shrines will be dedicated to the main deity the community worships.

Some Hindus visit their local mandir daily, whereas others only visit on special occasions, such as festivals. They bring offerings of flowers, food, milk or money and take off their shoes before they enter the central hall of the mandir.

Mandirs also have other important functions. They are a focal point for the local Hindu community, and provide educational and social facilities as well as being a place where Hindus can learn about their faith and worship.

## Arti

Arti is a ceremony in which love and devotion are offered to the deity. Worshippers are believed to receive their power and blessing in return. These rituals involve using symbols that represent the five elements of the universe: earth, air, fire, water and ether, from which Hindus believe everything was made.

A conch shell filled with water is blown at the beginning of the ceremony to represent water and ether. Offerings of incense and flowers signify the earth, and the waving of a fan represents air. The arti lamp, which has five lights on it, represents fire. During the service, the arti lamp is moved slowly in front of the deities.

*The Dakshineshwar Kali Temple in Calcutta, India*

# Havan

Havan is another important act of worship. It involves making an offering of fire to a deity. In a symbolic act of purification, the priest takes some holy water in his left hand, dips a finger from his right hand into it, and touches his ears, nose, eyes, mouth, arms, body and legs. The worshippers do the same while the priest says a **prayer** asking for power to be given to the five senses, and strength and energy to the limbs. He also prays for the good of human beings and offers prayers to the main deities. While chanting passages from the **Vedas**, the priest makes a small sacred fire. Ghee (clarified butter), **camphor**, grains and seeds are then offered to the deity.

*Hindus in India taking a blessing from the sacred flame during arti*

This is believed to invoke the power and blessing of the deities, which is passed on to the worshippers by them first cupping their hands over the flames, and then passing their hands over their eyes, forehead and hair. Devotees usually make a donation of money at this time.

At the end of the ceremony, worshippers are given **prashad**, a special mixture of food that has been blessed.

# Bhajans

Bhajans are devotional hymns or songs. They are one of the most popular ways in which Hindus express their feelings, beliefs and ideas about God. Musical instruments are played as an accompaniment and worshippers clap their hands in time to the singing.

Dance is another popular form of worship. Many young Hindus take dancing lessons, and specially trained dance groups perform dramatizations of well-known stories from Hindu scriptures.

## Learning about religion

❶ Make a list of reasons why Hindus might visit a mandir.

❷ Describe the main aspects of congregational worship in Hinduism and explain why they are important.

❸ 'What is the point of making an offering to God when everything belongs to God anyway?' Discuss this question in groups and report back to the rest of the class.

## Learning from religion

❶ What gift would you most like to give? To whom would you give it and why?

❷ Some people say that you should 'count your blessings' in times of difficulty. Explain what you think they mean by this and say how it could help.

❸ 'Dancing is for fun, not religion.' Do you agree with this statement? Give reasons for your answer.

# Festivals 1

## How is the Hindu calendar organized?

**Hinduism**, like most religions, has its own calendar. It is used to calculate the dates of festivals and favourable times for performing certain ceremonies. At one time, Hindus consulted several different calendars depending upon which part of India they lived in or came from. In 1957, the Indian government established one national calendar, which most Hindus living in India now use. Hindus living outside India use both the Hindu and **Gregorian calendars**. The Hindu calendar consists of three separate but interconnected and overlapping parts based on the movements of the sun and moon.

### The solar year

One solar year is 365 days and has twelve months. A leap year has 366 days. One solar month consists of the number of days it takes for the sun to move from one sign of the zodiac, or **rashi**, to another.

### The lunar year

A lunar year is generally also made up of twelve months. One lunar month consists of the number of days it takes for the moon to travel around the earth, approximately 29 solar days. However, because this leaves eleven solar days a year unaccounted for, Hindus add an extra month to the lunar year every three years.

A lunar month begins with the new moon and is divided into two fortnights. The first fortnight is the waxing of the moon, when more of it becomes visible. This is known as the bright fortnight. Many Hindus believe that this is a favourable time. The second fortnight is the waning of the moon, when its visibility decreases. This is known as the dark fortnight and is thought to be a less favourable time. The dates for most Hindu festivals are decided according to the phases of the moon.

### The twelve lunar months

| March/April | Chaitra |
|---|---|
| April/May | Vaisakha |
| May/June | Jyeshtha |
| June/July | Ashada |
| July/August | Shravan |
| August/September | Bhadrapad |
| September/October | Ashvin |
| October/November | Kartik |
| November/December | Margashirsha |
| December/January | Pausha |
| January/February | Magha |
| February/March | Phalguna |

## What role does astrology play in a Hindu's life?

Many Hindus believe that a person's life is affected by the positions of the stars and planets at the moment of birth. When a baby is born, an astrologer draws up a horoscope chart, or **Janmapatri**. Hindus believe that this chart can be used to highlight good and bad periods in

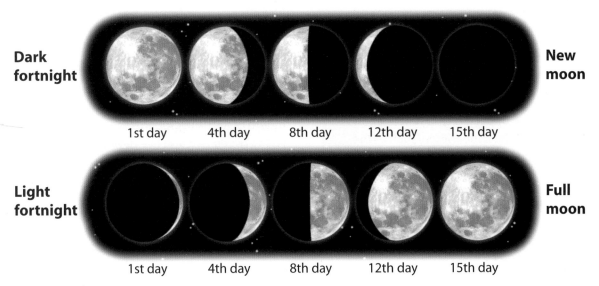

Dark fortnight

New moon

1st day    4th day    8th day    12th day    15th day

Light fortnight

Full moon

1st day    4th day    8th day    12th day    15th day

*The phases of the moon*

the baby's life and provide information about his or her character, occupation, marriage and any children he or she might have. It is also used to name the baby, and is looked at carefully before marriage to make sure that the bride and groom are matched astrologically.

| March/April | Aries/Mesha |
| April/May | Taurus/Vrishabha |
| May/June | Gemini/Mithuna |
| June/July | Cancer/Karkata |
| July/August | Leo/Simha |
| August/September | Virgo/Kanya |
| September/October | Libra/Tula |
| October/November | Scorpio/Vrischika |
| November/December | Sagittarius/Dhanur |
| December/January | Capricorn/Makara |
| January/February | Aquarius/Kumbha |
| February/March | Pisces/Mina |

*Rashis: the signs of the zodiac*

## Learning about religion

**1** Research the calendars the other five major world religions use. You could use the Internet to look for information.

**2** Explain the difference between the solar and lunar year, and say how they are divided.

**3** Describe the role astrology might play in a Hindu's life.

## Learning from religion

**1** Conduct a survey to find out which rashi applies to each member of your class and their attitude towards astrology. Make sure that you use the Hindu terms for each star sign and present your findings in a graph.

**2** In groups, brainstorm some well-known superstitions and discuss whether or not you agree with them.

**3** Describe your favourite time of the year and explain why you like it.

# Festivals 2

In this section you will:
- learn about some Hindu festivals
- have the opportunity to reflect upon some of the issues raised, such as the value of festivals, and your hopes and aspirations for the future.

## Which festivals do Hindus celebrate?

There are many festivals in **Hinduism**. Some Hindus think that some festivals are more important than others. This might be because of where they live or the **deity** they have chosen to worship. Hindu festivals are usually joyful occasions, but they have a serious side too. They are based on stories in Hindu scriptures, and have important religious and moral meanings. Most festivals take place annually and involve performing **puja**.

## Divali

One of the most important Hindu festivals is **Divali**, the festival of lights. It occurs in the month of Kartik (October/November), and can last between two and five days. Divali commemorates the Hindu New Year. Homes are cleaned and decorated with lights, either in the form of small electric light bulbs or **diva** lamps, clay lamps filled with oil and a floating cotton-wool wick. The creation of elaborate **rangoli** patterns on the ground is believed to encourage Lakshmi, the deity of good fortune, to visit and bring gifts of prosperity for the coming year.

Many Hindus see Divali as a time of renewal, or starting again. They try to make up any arguments and quarrels they have had, and put aside their differences with others. The festival coincides with the end of the financial year. Hindus try to settle their financial accounts at this time so that they do not enter the New Year in debt. This is also a popular time for consulting astrologers to see what may lie ahead in the next twelve months.

*A Hindu shrine lit up for Divali*

*During Navaratri, worshippers perform a variety of dances, some using sticks*

# Navaratri

The festival of Navaratri takes place in the month of Ashvin (September/October) and usually lasts for 'nine nights', which is the meaning of its name. The festival focuses on the Mother Goddess, who is worshipped primarily in the form of Durga. She is a fierce form of Shiva's consort, Parvati, and represents motherhood. One story Hindus remember at this time is when Durga killed a buffalo demon called Mahishasura. No man was able to defeat him, because Brahma had said he could only be killed by a woman.

On each night of the festival worshippers visit their local **mandir** and dance around a **shrine** dedicated to Durga. Worshippers may also say prayers for health and prosperity and they may **fast**, only eating fruit and sweet foods made with milk. Religions have different ideas about fasting. In Hinduism, it can mean going without certain everyday foods and replacing them with more unusual items.

# Dassehra

The festival of Dassehra directly follows Navaratri and its name means 'tenth day'.

This is when the **murti** of Durga worshipped during Navaratri is taken to a nearby river and washed. Hindus believe that this act symbolizes washing away all their unhappiness and bad luck. They believe that the energy of the Mother Goddess, given to them through Durga, can overcome evil and help them to transform their lives in a positive way.

The **Ramayana**, the story of Rama and Sita and Rama's victory over Ravana, is also remembered at this time. Many Hindu communities burn large images of the demon Ravana. This again demonstrates their belief that good will have victory over evil.

## Learning about religion

❶ Imagine you are a Hindu. Write a letter to a non-Hindu friend telling him or her how you celebrate Divali and what the festival means to you.

❷ Research the story of Durga slaying Mahishasura and make up a dance, which explains what happened, that Hindus could perform during Navaratri.

❸ Explain what a Hindu might be thinking or feeling as he or she watches the murti of Durga being washed in a river at the end of the festival of Dassehra.

## Learning from religion

❶ 'Festivals are for children.' Do you agree with this statement? Give reasons for your answer.

❷ Describe what you hope the next twelve months will bring for you and explain why.

❸ 'Evil flourishes when good men do nothing.' Discuss in pairs what you think this statement means.

# Festivals 3

In this section you will:

- learn more about some of the festivals Hindus celebrate
- have the opportunity to reflect upon and discuss some of the issues raised, such as celebrating birthdays and other important family occasions.

## Janmashtami

Janmashtami celebrates the birthday of Krishna, the eighth **avatar** of Vishnu. It occurs on the eighth day of the month of Shravan (July/August) and is a particularly important festival for the **devotees** of Vishnu. This is a time when Hindus evaluate their spiritual progress and decide how close they are to God.

In Hindu homes and **mandirs**, **murtis** of the infant Krishna are placed in cradles and swings. Hindus believe that Krishna was born at midnight, so they fast and stay up until that time.

When midnight arrives, they gather around the cradle or swing and greet Krishna by singing **bhajans**, dancing, and making offerings of food and sweets. An **arti** ceremony is also performed and **prashad**, a special combination of food that has been blessed, is shared out among the worshippers. Some mandirs organize non-stop readings of the **Bhagavad Gita** for eight days and nights preceding the festival. The readings are timed to finish at midnight, the time of Krishna's birth.

## Raksha Bandhan

*A cradle containing a murti of the infant Krishna. This is a focus for worship during Janmashtami*

*A young Hindu girl ties a rakhi on her brother's wrist during Raksha Bandhan*

The festival of Raksha Bandhan also takes place during the month of Sravana (July/August). During the festival, sisters thank their brothers for the love and protection they have shown them. They tie a **rakhi**, a coloured silk or cotton bracelet, around their brother's right wrist as a symbol of their gratitude. They are usually given a present in return. If a Hindu girl does not have a brother she can give a rakhi to one of her male cousins instead.

In some communities, Hindu girls are allowed to put a rakhi on any man's wrist and ask him to be their protector. Rakhis are also sent to various male relatives, brothers, cousins and nephews who live in other countries as a token of affection.

# Makara Sankranti

Makara Sankranti is based on the solar calendar. This means that the date of the festival is set according to the movements of the sun rather than the moon. It occurs around 14 January every year, when the sun passes from an area of the sky associated with one zodiac sign (Sagittarius/Dhanur) to the next (Capricorn/Makara). 'Makara' means 'Capricorn' and 'sankranti' refers to the day when the sun passes from one sign of the zodiac to the next. The sankranti of any month is considered important by Hindus and signifies a fresh start, but Makara Sankranti is thought to be a particularly special time. Hindus believe that anyone who dies on Makara Sankranti escapes **samsara**. This means that their **atman** is united with God and they will achieve **moksha**.

Hindus celebrate this festival in different ways, but the emphasis is on donating money to charities, and making up after arguments and quarrels. They also give each other sweets made with sesame seeds.

# Kumbh Mela

Kumbh Mela occurs every three years, with a special festival every twelve years, and is fixed according to the repetition of a particular astrological line-up of planets. The festival lasts for several weeks and is held in turn by four Indian cities: Allahabad, Hardwar, Ujjain and Nasik. All of these cities are situated close to **sacred** rivers and, during the course of the festival, millions of pilgrims bathe in the waters. Hindus believe that bathing in certain areas of the **Ganga** during Kumbh Mela will remove the effects of bad karma and will help them to achieve moksha. This means that they will no longer need to go through samsara: when they die they will be united with God.

## Learning about religion

❶ Explain why you think the festival of Janmashtami is particularly important for the devotees of Vishnu.

❷ Imagine that you are a journalist who has travelled to India for the Kumbh Mela festival. Research and write an article explaining the origins of the festival and why it is celebrated.

❸ In groups, produce a board game to teach younger children how and why Hindus celebrate different festivals.

## Learning from religion

❶ Discuss in groups how you would normally celebrate your birthday and how you would most like to celebrate your next birthday. Evaluate how and why people's ideas about celebrating birthdays might change as they become older.

❷ Describe your most important family occasion so far and explain why it was special to you.

❸ What festivals do you celebrate and why?

# Pilgrimage

## What is a pilgrimage?

A **pilgrimage** is a religious journey. It is also a form of worship. A person who goes on a pilgrimage is called a **pilgrim**. Pilgrims visit places they believe to be holy or **sacred**. A place might be considered holy or sacred if something of religious significance has happened there, such as a miraculous event or the birth of someone who is important to the religion. Sites of pilgrimage can also be found in a variety of natural locations. People can make pilgrimages on their own or go with others.

People go on pilgrimages for different reasons:

- to strengthen their faith and become closer to God
- to show commitment to their religion
- to say thank you for something good that has happened
- to make up for something they have done wrong
- to ask for help or healing
- to fulfil their religious duty
- to follow tradition
- to satisfy their curiosity.

Most Hindus believe that making a pilgrimage is part of their **dharma**, their religious duty. They believe that visiting sacred sites is one way to improve their **karma**. Many Hindus also believe that **prayers** said at pilgrimage sites are more effective.

## Where do Hindus go on pilgrimage?

India has hundreds of pilgrimage sites spread all over the country. Some of these places are significant for all Hindus, whereas others are only important to the **devotees** of a particular **deity**. Some Hindus believe that putting up with harsh conditions is part of what it means to serve God, and say that a pilgrimage has more spiritual value if a pilgrim walks to the site. There are usually **mandirs** and shrines at the most popular sacred places.

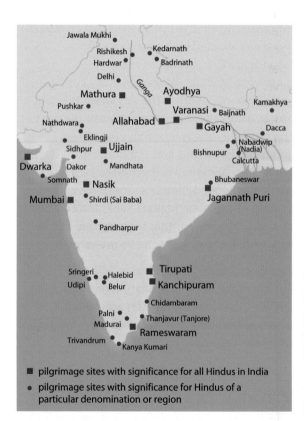

■ pilgrimage sites with significance for all Hindus in India

• pilgrimage sites with significance for Hindus of a particular denomination or region

*A map of India showing some important pilgrimage sites for Hindus*

## Varanasi

Varanasi, also known as Benares, attracts millions of pilgrims every year. Varanasi is associated with Shiva, a member of the **Trimurti** and the deity of destruction, who is said to have lived there for a time. It is also important to other religions besides **Hinduism**, and has been a centre for religious teaching and learning for thousands of years. The banks of the **Ganga** are lined with special platforms called ghats. Hindus believe that washing in this river will remove the effects of their bad karma, and make them spiritually clean.

O Mother Ganga [Ganges], I bow down to you.
By a mere touch of your holy waters,
even snakes, horses, deer and monkeys
(not to mention men) become as pure
and as beautiful as Shiva.
They can wander about unafraid.

Anon.

The ghats are also used for **cremation**. Many Hindus hope to die in Varanasi and have their ashes scattered on the Ganga. Hindus believe that this will enable them to achieve **moksha**, unity with God, and deliver them from **samsara**. A Hindu who dies at Varanasi and has his or her ashes scattered on the Ganga is said to have experienced the best death possible.

*A cremation by the banks of the Ganga at Varanasi*

## Vrindavan

Vrindavan is another sacred city. Hindus believe that it is the birthplace of Krishna, the eighth **avatar** of Vishnu. Pilgrims greet each other with the words 'Hare Krishna' and follow a special route around the city. They might also visit places in the surrounding area associated with Krishna's childhood and adolescence.

### Learning about religion

❶ Imagine that you are a Hindu asking for time off work to go on a pilgrimage to India. Write a dialogue between you and your boss in which you explain the reasons why this journey is important to you, and describe the cities or places you would like to visit and why.

❷ Explain why you think Hindus believe that someone who has died at Varanasi is said to have experienced the best death possible.

❸ Research some other sites of Hindu pilgrimage and present your findings in the form of a travel brochure for pilgrims. You could use the Internet to look for information.

### Learning from religion

❶ What city would you most like to visit and why?

❷ Write about an important journey you have made. Explain where you went and why it was special to you.

❸ 'How you have lived is more important than how you die.' Discuss this statement in groups.

# *Rites of passage 1*

## What are the Hindu rites of passage?

Rites of passage are special ceremonies that mark important stages in a person's life.

Traditionally, Hindus have four stages, or **ashramas**, in their lives. Each stage has religious rituals, called **samskars**, associated with it. There are sixteen samskars in total. The word 'samskar' means 'making perfect', and all of these ceremonies involve a purification rite where **prayers** are said for the individual concerned and his or her family. Details about how these rituals should be carried out are written down in Hindu scriptures. Many samskars are private family occasions and the rituals are performed at home, with or without a priest. The first samskar takes place before conception and the last one after death. Not all Hindus practise every one of the samskars and, for some Hindus, the time when the samskars are carried out varies.

The first nine samskars relate to childhood and begin before a baby is born.

The tenth, eleventh, twelfth, thirteenth and fourteenth samskars relate to youth.

The fifteenth samskar relates to middle age and is associated with marriage.

The sixteenth samskar relates to old age and is carried out after death.

Three samskars take place before birth. These ceremonies include the prospective parents praying for a healthy child and the foetus being read passages from Hindu scriptures.

The fourth samskar, called Jatakarman, takes place straight after birth. During the ceremony **mantras** are said, and the father or a priest feeds the baby a small amount of honey and ghee (clarified butter) using a gold object, such as a ring, pen or spoon. This is done in the hope that the child will be intelligent, and live a pure and good life.

Nowadays, many Hindus do not perform Jatakarman, or they combine it with the fifth samskar, the naming ceremony. The exact time of birth is noted and this information is used to draw up a horoscope chart, or **Janmapatri**, for the newborn baby. This chart is often consulted before further samskars take place.

The fifth samskar usually occurs about ten or twelve days after birth in the presence of friends and relatives. **Puja** is performed and the child is given several names. A priest or astrologer tells the parents which letter one of the child's names should begin with after looking at their Janmapatri.

The sixth samskar happens when the baby is taken on his or her first outing. Prayers are said to protect the child from the evil spirits that might exist outside the home.

The seventh samskar takes place when the baby eats solid food for the first time. A special mixture of rice is cooked while mantras from the **Vedas** are chanted. The child is given some of the food by either his father, a maternal uncle or a priest, while other members of the family watch. Puja is performed, and prayers are said in the hope that the child will live a good life and be happy, contented and strong.

The eighth samskar occurs when the child's ears are pierced. Prayers are said during the ceremony in hope that the child will be protected from disease.

The ninth samskar happens when the child has his or her first haircut. This is usually done by the father while mantras are said. Removing the child's hair symbolizes the elimination of any bad **karma** that has accumulated and been brought forward from a previous life, **samchita karma**.

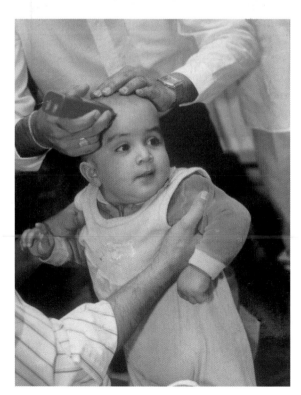

*The ninth samskar: a child's first haircut*

## Learning about religion

❶ Research the four ashramas and explain their significance for Hindus today. You could use the Internet to look for information.

❷ Draw a flow chart with illustrations explaining the first nine samskars.

❸ Compare and contrast how a Hindu upbringing might differ from a non-religious one. Use examples from the religion to support your statements.

## Learning from religion

❶ What stages in life do you think should be celebrated and why?

❷ Try to find out how and why your first name was chosen.

❸ 'Children should not take part in religious ceremonies until they are old enough to understand what is happening.' Do you agree? Give reasons for your answer. Use examples from the religions you have studied to support your statements.

## Upanayana – the sacred thread ceremony

The tenth **samskar** is a very important ceremony for boys who belong to the three highest **varnas**. It usually takes place between the ages of eight and twelve, and marks the beginning of a boy's religious life. This samskar is also known as **upanayana**, which means 'getting closer to God', or the **sacred** thread ceremony.

*The sacred thread ceremony is thought of as a spiritual birth. This is why males who belong to the three highest varnas are sometimes called 'twice-born'*

Part of the ceremony involves a sacred thread being draped over the boy's left shoulder. The thread has three strands, which represent three debts that the boy must now honour. The first debt is to God, the second debt is to his male ancestors and the third debt is to his **guru**, or spiritual teacher. The boy will wear the sacred thread for the rest of his life, only changing it at festivals, as a reminder of his **dharma**.

After upanayana, boys are able to carry out religious ceremonies. They are also expected to begin studying the Hindu scriptures under the guidance of a guru. Some boys spend several years studying and three further samskars might take place during this time.

## Marriage

The fifteenth samskar takes place when Hindus get married. It is one of the oldest and most significant rites of passage.

At the beginning of the wedding ceremony the couple place garlands around each others necks as symbols of acceptance. Then they sit side by side under a specially erected canopy facing the priest. **Prayers** are said for the couple and **mantras** from the **Vedas** are recited. The couple go on to make offerings of ghee (clarified butter) and grains into a sacred fire, which they walk around seven times while the priest, relatives and friends say prayers for their future happiness. For the first three rounds, the bride leads the groom and, for the next four, the groom leads the way. At the end of this they take seven steps together facing north. With each step, they pray for specific blessings such as food, happiness and strength. If the wedding takes place in India, the marriage is now legal and binding. Hindus living in other countries may also need to have a civil wedding if they want their marriage to be legally recognized.

*A Hindu bride and groom sitting under a specially erected wedding canopy. They are facing the priest*

# Death

The sixteenth samskar takes place after death. Hindus believe that this final rite of passage helps the **atman** to move on to the next life or phase of existence.

When someone dies, his or her body is washed and wrapped in a large piece of cloth, called a shroud. The corpse is then placed on a stretcher and carried to a **cremation** ground. This is usually done in a procession led by the deceased's eldest son or closest male relative, who carries a pot of water. Ideally, the place of cremation should be near one of India's seven sacred rivers or another source of running water.

The stretcher is placed on a funeral pyre and the nearest male relative of the person who has died walks around it three times sprinkling water. After he has done this he stands by head of the corpse and drops the pot so that it breaks. Hindus believe that this encourages the atman to be released from the body. Prayers are said and selected passages are read from Hindu scriptures. Ghee and sweet-smelling blocks of sandalwood are thrown on to the funeral pyre, which is lit and left to burn. The mourners return to collect the ashes later. They take the ashes and scatter them onto a river, preferably one of India's seven sacred rivers. After the funeral, there is a period of mourning, usually ten days, when the family restricts many of its activities such as cooking food at home. Nowadays, many Hindus, especially those living outside India, use modern crematoriums to dispose of the body, but the family of the deceased still try to take the ashes to India and have them sprinkled on the **Ganga**, if possible.

## Learning about religion

❶ Make a card you could send to a young Hindu boy on the occasion of his sacred thread ceremony. The card should show that you understand the religious significance of the event.

❷ Imagine you have been to a Hindu wedding. Write a letter to a friend describing what happened and why?

❸ Explain why you think Hindus practise cremation after death rather than burial.

## Learning from religion

❶ Discuss in pairs what duties or obligations you have towards people in your lives and the reasons for those duties.

❷ What blessings would you like to give a newly married couple and why?

❸ Imagine that you are a human resources manager for a large company. You need to decide upon a policy for staff absence in the event of the death of a close relative. Prepare a report explaining how an official period of mourning might help the relatives of someone who has died.

# *Creation 1*

## What do Hindus believe about creation?

Hindus believe that God, in the form of Brahma, is the creator of the universe and everything in it. However, they have different beliefs and ideas about how this actually happened. There are numerous creation **myths** in **Hinduism** that describe some aspects of creation, but there is nothing to say exactly how everything began in the first place. Many Hindus accept that this is a mystery and think it is impossible to know how the universe came into existence.

Then even nothingness was not, nor existence.
There was no air then, nor the heavens
     beyond it.
Who covered it? Where was it? In whose
     keeping?
Was there then cosmic water, in depths
     unfathomed?
But, after all, who knows, and who can say,
Whence it all came, and how creation
     happened?
The deities themselves are later than creation,
So who knows truly when it has arisen?

                                        Rig Veda, X, 129

A myth is a story that describes mysterious events, unusual traditions or extraordinary sights in nature. They are usually ancient and have been passed on by word of mouth for hundreds of years before being written down.

One of the most well-known Hindu creation myths is a hymn found in the **Vedas**. It says that everything in creation is the result of the sacrifice of Purusha, the first man. The sacrifice resulted in ghee being produced which was made into the birds and creatures that live on the earth, and into the **deities**, the sun and moon. The atmosphere came from Purusha's naval; his head formed the heaven; his feet produced the earth; and the sky came from his ear. Purusha is also said to have been responsible for the four **varnas**. The **Brahmins** came from his mouth, the **Kshatriyas** from his arms, the **Vaishyas** from his thighs, and the **Shudras** from his feet. When taken literally, this story contradicts the modern theory of **evolution**, the idea that everything in the universe developed gradually over a long period of time.

### Learning about religion

❶ Describe and explain the Hindu attitude towards creation.

❷ Research the creation stories of other religions. Compare and contrast them with Hinduism.

❸ 'If the notion of creation cannot be proved, how do we know whether God exists or not?' How might a Hindu respond to this statement?

### Learning from religion

❶ Discuss in groups where you think human beings came from and report back to the rest of your class.

❷ Can you create something from nothing? Give reasons for your answer.

❸ Write a poem about an aspect of creation that interests or puzzles you.

The Supreme Lord, in the form of the universe, has a thousand heads, a thousand eyes and a thousand feet, for He contains all the living entities.

The universes, past, present and future, are but manifestations of the Supreme Lord who expands Himself as the Purusha. He is the Lord of immortality but has manifest Himself as the Purusha in the universe.

The past, present and future universes are manifestations of the Lord's powers, but the Lord Himself is much greater.

The Lord began the work of creation, by going all around, taking the form of all animate and inanimate objects.

From that Lord, the universe was born, and in that the Virat Purusha, Paramatman of the universe, was born. Having appeared, the Virat Purusha grew, and produced the earth and the bodies of the jivas.

The Devas, being the first beings manifested, performed a mental sacrifice to complete the creation with an offering. Spring was the ghee, summer was the fuel, wood, and autumn was the offering.

In this sacrifice, the kusha-grass blades strewn around the fire (for protection from Rakshasas) were seven (the seven Vedic poetic metres), and the fuel sticks were twenty-one (twelve months, six seasons and the three worlds).

The Devas, Sadhyas and Rishis, placed the Virat Purusha, the first being of the universe, on kusha and sprinkled Him with water for purification. In this way they conducted the mental sacrifice using the Virat Purusha.

From that sacrifice where everything in the universe was sacrificed, yoghurt and ghee (all nourishing foods) were produced. It created the animals of the air, forest, and village.

From that ultimate sacrifice the Rik (hymns), Sama (musical) and Yajus (prose) portions of the Vedas were born.

From the sacrifice horses were born, and animals with two sets of teeth such as donkeys and mules. From the sacrifice, cows were born, and likewise goats and sheep.

From the face came the Brahmins. From the two arms the Kshatriyas came into being. From the thighs of the Virat Purusha came the Vaishyas and from His feet the Shudras were born.

The moon was born from His mind, the Sun was born from His two eyes. From His mouth were born Indra and Agni, and from His breath Vayu was born.

From His navel came the antariksa (space between earth and heaven). From His head the heavens arose. From His feet the earth arose and from His ears arose the directions. In this way the worlds were created.

Brahma explained his realization to Indra. Indra, who knows all the living entities in all four directions, explained it to all others. One who knows the nature of the Virat Purusha becomes immortal even in his life on earth. There is no other path to reach the goal of immortality.

**Extracts from the Rig Veda**

# Creation 2

In this section you will:

- learn more about Hindu beliefs about creation
- find out about the Hindu attitude towards the environment
- have the opportunity to express your own views on ecological issues and research the work of organizations who campaign to protect the environment.

## The avatars of Vishnu

Some Hindus believe that the nine **avatars** of Vishnu can help to explain creation. They say that each of his incarnations represents a stage in **evolution**. **Hinduism** also teaches that each of Vishnu's avatars is associated with a particular period of time on earth.

## What is the Hindu attitude towards the environment?

We may utilize the gifts of nature just as we choose, but in her books, the debits are always equal to the credits.
The earth provides enough to satisfy everyone's needs, but not everyone's greed.

Mahatma Gandhi

Hinduism teaches that human beings should respect and live in harmony with nature. It teaches that the earth's resources are a gift from God, and should be used responsibly and unselfishly. A balance must be kept between what is taken from the earth and what is replenished.

Natural places such as the banks of rivers, mountains, coastlines and seashores are considered holy. Trees are also thought to be **sacred**. It is considered an act of goodness to plant and water them. Many religious rituals surround the planting and cutting of trees. Trees are only cut down when absolutely necessary and the trees are asked for forgiveness before this is done. Many Hindus are environmentalists, and campaign against deforestation and other ecological issues.

## Learning about religion

1. Summarize the avatars of Vishnu and explain why you think some Hindus say that they support the theory of evolution.

2. Discuss in pairs what you think Mahatma Gandhi was saying about how human beings should treat the environment. Produce an environmentally-friendly slogan that he might have agreed with.

3. Analyze and account for different religious opinions concerning the use of the environment. Use examples from religions you have studied to support your statements.

## Learning from religion

1. Research one environmental organization and prepare an information leaflet about its current campaigns.

2. Produce a poster encouraging people to care for the environment.

3. Imagine that you have been invited to speak at an ecological conference. Prepare a statement about how you believe people should treat the environment and explain why you think this way.

1. In his first avatar Vishnu appeared as a giant fish called Matsya. A previous creation of human beings had ended because they had all been wicked. Everyone had drowned except the king and seven wise men and their families, who had taken pairs of different animals on to an ark. Matsya towed the ark to safety and a new creation was established.

10. Hindus believe that there is a tenth avatar yet to come and that, after some time, Vishnu will recreate the world.

2. As Kurma, a giant tortoise, he carried a giant mountain on his back. This acted as a pivot for the instrument the **deities** used to churn the sea in the search for the ambrosia (divine nectar) needed to restore power to the deities, headed by Indra. Kumbh Mela remembers this event.

9. As Buddha, the enlightened one, Vishnu teaches **ahimsa**, or non-violence, towards all living things. Some Hindus believe that the teachings of the Buddha can help a person to achieve **moksha**.

3. As Varaha, a giant boar, Vishnu saved the earth from a second flood. He dived into the sea and brought the earth up out of the water by balancing it on his two tusks.

8. As Krishna, Vishnu, had many wonderful adventures, which inspire his **devotees** and encourage them to live according to their **dharma**.

4. As Narasimha, half-man and half-lion, Vishnu killed Hiranyaksipu, who tortured his son Prahlad. Hiranyaksipu could not be killed by any human being or animal or by any weapon, so Vishnu appeared as half-man and half-lion, and killed him with his nails.

7. As Rama, the hero of the **Ramayana**, Vishnu defeated a ten-headed demon called Ravana. This event is remembered at **Divali** and Dassehra.

5. As Vamana, a dwarf, Vishnu saved the deities from a demon king called Bali. He tricked Bali into handing over his kingdom by asking for three steps of land. Thinking that Vamana was small, Bali agreed to his request. Vishnu then expanded his size so that his steps covered the entire universe.

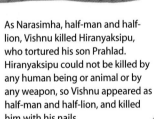

6. As Parasurama, Rama in another form, Vishnu saved human society from wicked kings and rulers (**Kshatriyas**) who were abusing their power and not following religious teachings.

*The avatars of Vishnu*

51

# Moral issues 1

*A Hindu will often talk to their priest or guru before making an important decision*

In this section you will:

- learn how Hindus decide what is right and what is wrong
- find out about the Hindu attitude to animal rights
- have the opportunity to express your own views on these issues.

## What is a moral issue?

Morality is about right and wrong behaviour. A **moral** issue is a situation that might be considered to be right or wrong for a variety of reasons, for example, because of the laws of a country, the teachings of a religion, or the beliefs and values of an individual or community. A moral decision is where a choice has to be made between what is the right thing to do and the wrong thing to do. Not all the decisions people have to make are moral decisions.

The word '**immoral**' means 'wrong'. An immoral act is an action that is thought to be morally wrong. This means that it is an unacceptable way to behave.

The word '**amoral**' means 'without moral standards or principles'. Someone who is amoral shows no understanding of what is right or wrong.

## How do Hindus decide what is right and wrong?

Hindus try to live their lives in the way they believe God wants. They think that fulfilling their **dharma** will help them to achieve **moksha**. Hindus believe that the experiences of the **deities**, **gurus** and other holy men, such as **swamis** and priests, can show them the right way to live. When making a moral decision, many Hindus think about what their favourite or

special deity would do in a similar situation, and may pray to them for help and advice. They might also consider what their guru and the priest of their local **mandir** would have to say about the issue. They may ask the advice of other Hindus.

*Just try to learn the truth by approaching a spiritual master. Inquire from him submissively and render service unto him. The self-realized souls can impart knowledge to you because they have seen the truth.*

**Bhagavad Gita**, 4, 34

Hindus can find out what the various deities might have done by reading stories about them in **sacred** scriptures. These holy books also contain important moral teachings about the right and wrong way to behave. They are a source of moral authority for most Hindus. A source of moral authority is something or someone telling a person what to do in moral situations.

*But ignorant and faithless persons who doubt the revealed scriptures do not attain God consciousness; they fall down. For the doubting soul there is happiness neither in this world nor in the next.*

Bhagavad Gita, 4, 41

Another important consideration for Hindus would be whether their actions would result in good or bad **karma**. Karma is the belief that all thoughts and actions have results which correspond to them.

Hindus believe that ultimately people will bear the consequences of their deeds. This means that their behaviour during one lifetime will determine the quality of their next life. If they behave well and live according to their dharma, their next life will better than the one they have now. They will be one or more stages nearer to achieving moksha. The reverse is also true: if people behave badly and do not live according to their dharma, their next life will be worse than the one they have now. They will be further away from achieving moksha.

## What do Hindus think about animal rights?

*Hindus believe that the cow is a sacred animal. They say that the cow acts as a mother to human beings because she supplies them with her milk, which nourishes them and keeps them healthy. The **Vedas** specifically forbid the killing of cows*

**Hinduism** teaches that the greatest dharma is to practise **ahimsa**. The idea of ahimsa comes from the belief that God gives life to all living creatures, and human beings have no right to destroy it. It means having reverence and empathy for all forms of life. Most Hindus are vegetarians because of this belief.

Hindus also treat animals with respect because they believe that there is a part of God in every living thing. In human beings and animals this forms the **atman**. According to the principles of **samsara**, the atman can experience life as an animal if there is bad karma carried over from its previous existence.

### Learning about religion

❶ Explain the difference between a moral and an immoral act using examples to support your definitions.

❷ Describe the process a Hindu might go through when making a moral decision.

❸ Role-play a Hindu and a non-Hindu discussing the issue of animal rights.

### Learning from religion

❶ Discuss in groups how you decide what is right and what is wrong.

❷ Prepare a report that analyzes and accounts for different views concerning animal rights.

❸ 'We call them dumb animals, and so they are, for they cannot tell us how they feel, but they do not suffer less because they have no words.' (Anna Sewell, *Black Beauty*, 1877)

If animals could talk, what do you think they would say about the way they are treated?

# Moral issues 2

## Prejudice and discrimination

Prejudice is when you prejudge someone. This means that you form an opinion about a person without knowing what he or she is like. Discrimination is when you act on your prejudice and treat some people better or worse than others because of what you believe to be true about them. There are many different kinds of prejudice, and people can be discriminated against for a variety of reasons, such as size, accent, colour, gender, age, ability and race. Discrimination on the basis of race or colour is known as racism. Treating people the same way regardless of their status, physical characteristics or mental abilities is called equality.

Prejudice can lead to stereotyping. This is when you form fixed mental images about what a particular group of people are like. Stereotyping assumes that every member of a group is the same and will act the same way.

## How do Hindus believe people should treat each other?

**Hinduism** teaches that that all human beings should be treated with respect because they have part of God within them, in the form of their **atman**. A traditional greeting used by most Hindus, regardless of age, sex or **caste**, demonstrate this belief. It is called 'Namaste', which literally means 'I honour that place in you where God resides.' The phrase is said with the palms of the hands together and a slight bow from the waist. This greeting symbolizes respect and acknowledges the presence of God in another human being.

Hinduism is also tolerant of other religions and races. However, because of beliefs associated with their religion, Hindus have not always treated each other with respect. This has led to inequality, prejudice and discrimination within the religion (see the section on Hindu society, pages 26–7).

## Mahatma Gandhi

During the early part of the twentieth century, Mahatma Gandhi, an important Hindu leader, campaigned against the idea of 'untouchability' and the injustice of the caste system in general. He renamed the untouchables harijans, 'children of God'. Gandhi believed that there was only one God and that people should not be divided or discriminated against because of their religion. As part of his campaign, Gandhi established an **ashram**, a community to encourage spiritual development, where Hindus of all castes and harijans lived and worked together. One of the important features of this community was that everyone took turns at doing various jobs.

My religion is Hinduism which, for me, is the religion of humanity and includes the best of all the religions known to me.
Mine is not a religion of the prison house. It has room for the least among God's creations. But it is a proof against insolence, pride of race, religion and colour.

Mahatma Gandhi

*Mahatma Gandhi outside the Sabarmati Ashram, Ahmedabad, India*

The 'untouchables' now refer to themselves as **dalits**, 'the oppressed'. They have formed a political party and continue to campaign for a more equal society. In other countries, such as the UK, many Hindus associate with and marry people outside of their own caste and **varna**. The modern way of life has led to the breakdown of many traditional social barriers.

The efforts of Gandhi and others eventually led to a law being passed by the Indian government in 1948 which banned untouchability. Other legislation followed to try and ensure equality for all of the citizens of India.

**Right to Equality**

Equality before law. Prohibition of discrimination on grounds of religion, race, caste, sex or place of birth. Equality of opportunity in matters of public employment. Abolition of untouchability. Abolition of titles. Right to freedom. Protection of certain rights regarding freedom of speech, etc. Protection in respect of conviction for offences. Protection of life and personal liberty. Protection against arrest and detention in certain cases.

From the Indian Constitution 1948

## Learning about religion

1. Explain how religion can lead to prejudice and discrimination using examples to support your statements. Suggest how fairness and equality could be achieved.

2. Think carefully about what religious people might need to develop their relationship with God. Design your own purpose-built community for spiritual development. Explain the significance of the features you have chosen.

3. In groups, research and produce a 'This was your life' presentation for Mahatma Gandhi. You could use the Internet to look for relevant information.

## Learning from religion

1. Make a list of the different ways you can let some know that he or she is valued and respected.

2. How do you believe people should treat each other? Give reasons for your answer.

3. In pairs, plan a campaign to promote equality for all of the citizens in the country in which you live. State what actions you would take and why?

# *Ultimate questions 1*

In this section you will:

- explore some Hindu responses to ultimate questions
- have the opportunity to think about how the existence of God could help to explain some of life's mysteries
- express your own views on why we exist, and the purpose and meaning of life.

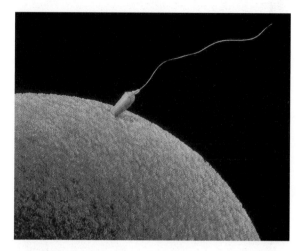

*A new life begins – an egg and sperm at the point of fertilization*

Ultimate questions are important questions to which there are no definite or absolute answers, for example, 'Does God exist?' or 'How did everything begin?' People often ask ultimate questions to try to make sense of the world in which they live, or to find purpose and meaning in their lives. There are many things in life that cannot easily be explained and the way in which people respond to ultimate questions depends on their world-view. Many people believe that the existence of God can explain these mysteries.

**Hinduism** teaches that asking ultimate questions is an important part of a person's spiritual development. Many Hindus believe that everything a person does is pointless unless the person asks questions about God and their place in the world.

## Why do we exist?

Hindus believe that all life is a precious gift from God. They say that we exist because God has chosen to give us life. The idea that all life is **sacred** because it comes from God is called the sanctity of life. The Hindu belief in the sanctity of life is expressed as **ahimsa**. This means not injuring any living creature by thought, word or deed. Belief in ahimsa affects how Hindus deal with issues such as genetic engineering, embryo technology, abortion and euthanasia.

## What are we here for?

Hindus believe that human beings are born in a state of ignorance about their real purpose in life. This is why spiritual teachers are thought to be important because they 'awaken' individuals to the true meaning of existence on earth. Once awakened, Hindus see that their purpose in life is to develop spiritually and to show their love for God. To do this properly, they must fulfill their **dharma**, which involves helping and caring for other people. Giving loving service to God and human beings is known as **seva**. According to Hindu scriptures it is the highest form of dharma. Some seva can produce good **karma**, which enables the **atman** to proceed towards **moksha** where it will be united with God. There are many ways Hindus can perform seva – for example, by worshipping regularly or by giving time and money to noble causes.

## What happens when we die?

For to one that is born death is certain,
And birth is certain for one that has died;

enough spiritual credit to be permanently united with God.

The state of being united with God after death is known as moksha, which means that the atman no longer needs to go through **samsara**. Hindus see this as a welcome release from the frustration and suffering associated with life on earth.

*Hindus helping each other at a community health programme in Rajasthan, India*

Therefore, the thing being unavoidable,
Thou shouldst not mourn.
The embodied [soul] is eternally unslayable
In the body of everyone.
**Bhagavad Gita** 2, 27 and 30

Hindus believe that the atman is eternal. This means that the atman continues to exist after death and takes on another form of existence. This next form is determined by its **samchita karma**. The atman will either enjoy or suffer the results of thoughts and actions during former human existences. **Hinduism** teaches that every living being has an eternal relationship with God, called **svarupa**, which is remembered and restored through devotional service to God and others. However, it may take many lifetimes before the atman has overcome the effect of negative and selfish activities and earned

## Learning about religion

❶ Describe how a belief in the sanctity of life could affect a person's attitude towards genetic engineering, embryo technology, abortion and euthanasia. Use examples from the religions you have studied to support your answers.

❷ 'Everything happens for a reason.' Explain how might a Hindu respond to this statement?

❸ Write a dialogue between a Hindu and a Christian discussing their beliefs about life after death. Your conversation should explain the differences and similarities between their points of view.

## Learning from religion

❶ Write down an ultimate question you would like to know the answer to and give it to a partner to answer. Discuss your partner's response and say whether or not you agree with it and why.

❷ 'Life is for living, not asking questions.' Do you agree? Give reasons for your answer.

❸ Write a poem that expresses your views about life after death.

In this section you will:

- look at how Hindus respond to the problems of evil and suffering

- have the opportunity to reflect upon some of the issues raised, such as the existence of God, the origins of evil and helping others.

## Where does suffering come from?

There are many different causes of suffering. Sometimes suffering occurs as a result of a natural disaster, such as an earthquake or flooding. It is described as 'natural' because it does not seem to result from human action.

Suffering can also be caused by human beings through deliberate acts of violence, for example, murder, terrorism and war. This kind of suffering is the result of human-made or moral evil. The word 'evil' means 'wrong' or 'wicked'. We say something is evil when it causes harm or injury to living beings. Moral evil is when the suffering is caused by deliberate human actions.

Not all causes of suffering fit into these two categories. For example, human beings sometimes cause suffering to others accidentally, and some natural disasters are the result of humans misusing or abusing natural resources.

## What is the Hindu response to suffering?

Hindus believe that there are reasons for the presence of pain and suffering in the world. They say that the pain and suffering experienced on earth is the result of bad **samchita karma** (accumulated karma). Karma is seen as the

*Refugees receiving hospitality in a Hindu community in Charlestown, South Africa*

ultimate justice for good and evil behaviour. Nevertheless, Hindus still find suffering and pain difficult to deal with, and the aim of every Hindu is to be liberated from **samsara** so that they no longer have to endure it.

Many Hindus also work hard to try to alleviate the sufferings of others. They see it as part of their **dharma**, religious duty. The Ramakrishna Vedanta Mission was founded in order to promote spiritual development and to provide social services to the poor and deprived in India. The motto of the organization is 'Liberation for oneself and service to mankind'.

# The Ramakrishna Vedanta Mission

The Ramakrishna Vedanta Mission has its own hospitals, maternity clinics, tuberculosis clinics and mobile dispensaries, and it maintains training centres for nurses. The Mission also runs orphanages and homes for the elderly, and carries out rural and tribal welfare work.

In educational activities, the Ramakrishna Vedanta Mission has consistently been ahead of its time. It has developed some of the most outstanding educational institutions in India, having its own colleges, vocational training centres, high schools and primary schools, and teacher training institutes, as well as schools for partially sighted people. The Mission also runs adult education centres throughout the county.

Whenever disaster strikes, the Ramakrishna Vedanta Mission is there to offer relief from famine, epidemic, fire, flood, earthquake, cyclone and communal disturbances.

## Learning about religion

❶ 'The existence of evil and suffering are two very good reasons for not believing in God.' Role-play, in groups, an atheist, an agnostic and a theist discussing this statement.

❷ Describe and explain the Hindu attitude towards suffering.

❸ 'God knows, but does God care'. Explain what you think this statement means and how it relates to different religious ideas about suffering and evil.

## Learning from religion

❶ Analyze and account for different opinions concerning the origins of evil and the presence of suffering in the world.

❷ Imagine that you are setting up a new organization that aims to relieve suffering and evil in the world. What would your priority be and why?

❸ 'You should not worry about other people. They cannot get into any more trouble than they deserve.' Do you agree? Give reasons for your answer.

*The logo of the Ramakrishna Vedanta Mission*

# Glossary

**Ahimsa** 'not killing', 'non-violence'; a reverence and respect for all life

**Amoral** without moral qualities, characteristics

**Arti** a religious ceremony during which love and devotion are offered to the deity, and the worshippers believe they receive blessings and power from the deity in return

**Asceticism** choosing to live a simple and harsh life for religious reasons

**Ashram** a community set up for spiritual development

**Ashrama** a stage of life; there are four of these

**Atman** the soul or 'real self', a part of God that is in all living beings

**Aum** (Om) a sacred sound and symbol that represents God

**Avatar** 'one who descends'; refers to the appearance or incarnation of a deity on earth, usually Vishnu

**Bhagavad Gita** 'The Song of the Lord'; part of the Mahabharata, believed to have been spoken by Krishna, and one of the most popular Hindu sacred texts

**Bhagavad Purana** a collection of twelve books containing information about the avatars of Vishnu and famous stories about Krishna

**Bhajans** devotional hymns or songs

**Brahmin** the first of the four varnas. Priests come from this varna

**Camphor** an aromatic substance believed to have antiseptic properties. It is burnt and used as a disinfectant in order to cleanse and purify the air around a place of prayer such as a shrine

**Caste** a sub-group within a varna made up of numerous families who follow the same occupation. Also known as a jati

**Caste system** the organization of Indian society into occupational kinship groups

**Cremation** the burning of a dead body

**Dalit** 'the oppressed'; a name adopted by Hindus who are outside the caste system. They are also known as 'untouchables' or harijans, 'children of God'

**Deity** a god or goddess

**Denomination** a group within Hinduism

**Devotees** dedicated followers of a religion, or worshippers of a particular deity

**Dharma** religion or religious duty

**Diva** a small clay oil-filled lamp with a floating wick, used at the festival of Divali

**Divali** a festival of lights that commemorates the Hindu New Year

**Divine** godlike

**Evolution** the gradual and natural development of the universe over a long period of time

**Fast** to stop eating all or certain foods, especially for religious reasons

**Ganga** also known as the Ganges, the most famous of all the sacred rivers in India

**Gregorian calendar** a calendar commonly used in Christian countries. The calendar takes Jesus' birth as its starting point. According to the Gregorian calendar, a year is 365.2425 days. Every fourth year, called a leap year, an extra day (29 February) is added to the calendar

**Guru** a spiritual teacher, also known as a sadhu, swami or holy man

**Henotheistic** the worship of only one deity as the Supreme God

**Hermit** a person who lives in solitude

**Hinduism** a major world religion, also known as Sanatan Dharma, the eternal or imperishable religion

**Immoral** unacceptable, wrong behaviour

**Janmapatri** a horoscope chart drawn up by an astrologer, usually for a newborn baby

**Jati** a sub-group within a varna made up of numerous families who follow the same occupation. Also known as a caste

**Karma** 'action'; the law of cause and effect. The belief that all thoughts and actions have results that correspond to them

**Kshatriyas** the second of the four varnas, made up of rulers and soldiers

**Lotus** a flower used as a symbol to represent purity and goodness

**Mahabharata** the world's longest poem, a sacred text also known as the Great Indian Epic, which includes the Bhagavad Gita

**Mala** a string of wooden prayer beads used in meditation, also known as a rosary

**Mandir** Hindu place of worship, also known as a temple

**Mantra**  a short religious saying or prayer that devotees chant regularly as part of their worship

**Maya**  'illusory', 'finite'; something that does not last forever

**Meditation**  a form of quiet prayer that involves clearing the mind of all distractions and concentrating on God

**Moksha**  liberation or freedom from samsara

**Monotheistic**  a belief in one God

**Moral**  conforming to accepted good standards of general behaviour

**Murti**  an image or representation of a deity

**Myths**  ancient stories about mysterious events, unusual traditions or extraordinary sights in nature

**Pilgrim**  a person who goes on a religious journey or pilgrimage

**Pilgrimage**  a religious journey

**Prashad**  sacred, blessed food, given to worshippers at the end of some religious ceremonies. It usually consists of fruit, nuts and crystallized sugar

**Prayer**  a way of approaching or communicating with God; a form of worship

**Puja**  worship. A general term referring to a variety of practices in the home or the mandir

**Puranas**  a collection of Hindu sacred texts that contain stories about Brahma, Vishnu and Shiva, and teachings about morality. The most important Purana is the Bhagavad Purana

**Rakhi**  a bracelet made out of coloured cotton or silk, given to some male Hindus, usually brothers, as a symbol of gratitude and protection

**Ramayana**  a sacred text in the form of a poem which tells the story of Rama and Sita

**Rangoli**  repetitive, geometrical patterns which are painted in coloured powder; a traditional art of India

**Rashi**  sign of the Hindu zodiac

**Reincarnation**  samsara, the cycle of birth, death and rebirth

**Sacred**  holy, associated with God

**Saint**  someone who has been recognized after his or her death as being especially holy and dedicated to God while alive

**Samchita karma**  the combined consequences of a person's thoughts and actions, which are carried over from one lifetime to another

**Samsara**  reincarnation, the cycle of birth, death and rebirth

**Samskars**  sixteen religious ceremonies that mark important stages in a Hindu's life

**Sanatan Dharma**  the eternal or imperishable religion, also known as Hinduism

**Sanskrit**  one of the world's oldest languages and the original language in which many Hindu scriptures were written

**Seva**  service either to God or to human beings

**Shaivas**  people who worship Shiva as the Supreme God

**Shaktas**  people who worship Shakta, the wife of Shiva, in one of her various forms such as Durga or Kali, as the Supreme God

**Shakti**  the destructive and reproductive energy associated with Shiva, which usually takes the form of a female deity

**Shrine**  a special place set aside for worship

**Shruti**  'that which is heard'; 'divinely given'; a category of sacred writing believed to have been composed by God

**Shudras**  the lowest of the four varnas, made up of unskilled workers

**Smriti**  'that which has been remembered'; a category of sacred writing believed to have been composed by realized souls, souls which have achieved moksha

**Svarupa**  a term used to describe the eternal relationship between living beings and God

**Swami**  a spiritual teacher also known as a guru, sadhu or holy man

**Swastika**  'well-being'; a favourable Hindu symbol that represents good fortune and happiness

**Transmigration**  the belief that the atman, or soul, survives after death and enters a new body

**Trimurti**  the three main forms of God: Brahma (the Creator), Vishnu (the Preserver) and Shiva (the Destroyer)

**Upanayana**  the sacred thread ceremony, the tenth samskar. A very important religious ceremony for boys who belong to the three highest varnas

**Vaishnavas**  people who worship Vishnu and his avatars as the Supreme God

**Vaishyas**  the third of the four varnas, made up of merchants (shopkeepers and traders) and farmers

**Varnas**  four classes or groups that make up traditional Indian society

**Vedas**  'to know', 'knowledge'; a collection of shruti, 'divinely given writings'. The oldest and most important Hindu sacred writings

# Index